"A powerful, prophetic master[...] into the hearts of fathers and children around the world! This desperately needed book divinely bridges the gap between the generations and allows spiritual transfer for lasting spiritual legacy!"

—*Bishop Dale C. Bronner, D. Min.*
Senior pastor, Word of Faith Family Worship Cathedral
Author, *Change Your Trajectory*

"Doug Stringer clearly paints a picture of the role of a father in a child or teen's life and the effects that the absence of fathers are having on this generation. May the following pages inspire you to aggressively pursue and win your own children's hearts for God."

—*Ron Luce*
Founder, Teen Mania Ministries

"Sacrifice is never about death; it is always about life. The sacrifice at the cross was about life and redemption for the entire world. Seldom does one see in their own circle of friends sacrifice made that could shift the future of nations. One of my closest friends has made that sacrifice for decades...Doug Stringer. From the day he met Jesus as a successful entrepreneur Doug started caring for people. In his passionate love for Christ he started taking in addicts from the streets—seventeen of them at one point—and housed them in his little apartment. Nobody told him to do that. That's just Doug. And, decades later, it's still Doug. This book isn't just words; it's a lifestyle that will transform your life and change the world around you. It's the lifestyle of pursuing the Father's blessing."

—*Paul Louis Cole, D.Th.*
President, Christian Men's Network Worldwide
Global Fatherhood Initiative

"This book comes not just from Doug's life experiences, but from the person whom God has molded Doug to be. He doesn't just write about investing in people, he lives it. Doug's communication style has always been 'straight talk, with huge lashings of love.' Definitely recommended reading."

—*Andrew Merry*
National Field Experience Coordinator
Compassion International–Australia

"I had no idea this book would touch a deep chord in my heart. From the stories Doug tells to his amazing biblical insight, I was moved to tears, smiles, and even healing. I believe everyone will gain a closer relationship with the Father through the pages of this book. Thank you, Doug!"

—*Lisa Abbott*
Film producer and entertainment distributor

"Doug Stringer is wonderfully qualified to share tender, sensitive words that can bring healing and transformation to those who desire it. I recommend this book to all who struggle with issues dealing with their fathers—and also for those who do not."

—*Dr. Paul Cedar*
Chairman, Mission America Coalition

"A handbook for fulfilling the destiny of two generations of fathers and sons: the Elijahs and the Elishas, the Pauls and the Timothys. Doug's life is a testimony to an entire generation that struggles to fit in with orthodox American Christianity. It is Doug's passion for God and his authentic love as an apostolic father that has pioneered a path for today's emerging leaders."

—*Matt Stevens*
Director, Somebody Cares Baltimore

"Wow! Talk about a book that makes you experience the whole spectrum of emotions! I first had a deep, aching in my heart and sadness for the state of our generation, then found myself wanting to jump up and down and say, 'Here I am, send me!' Doug loves us enough to be honest with us about our desperate situation but doesn't leave us scratching our heads over how to solve it. He provides the answers and the direction, based on God's Word."

—*Kimiko Soldati*
US Olympic Diver

"Doug Stringer has come through personal pain into a place of victory, and God has commissioned him as a courageous and insightful instrument of healing for the fatherless—naturally and spiritually. His sensitivity in addressing this difficult subject demonstrates the Lord's tender compassion toward the abandoned and broken-hearted. This is not just a message Doug preaches and writes about; it is one he lives."

—*Brenda J. Davis*
Former editor, *SpiritLed Woman*

"*In Search of a Father's Blessing* will not only heal the relationship gulf between fathers and sons in the body of Christ, but it will be the needle and thread to mend the tear between fathers and sons in the secular world, as well. As fathers, we must pass on a better world to our children. And in order to pass the baton to the next generation, we must be able to run alongside them."

—*Dr. Ed Montgomery*
Pastor, Abundant Life Cathedral, Houston, Texas

"*In Search of a Father's Blessing* is so relevant to what is going on now in our world. I started reading it and couldn't put it down. In my ministry, I talk a lot about absent fathers but I was still amazed with some of the statistics I read. I've already been put in situations in which I used this book to minister to people. So many people have relationships with God the Father that are messed up because they don't have a relationship with their earthly father. I pray that people all over the world will read this message and will be convicted but also inspired."

—*Melvin Adams*
Former Harlem Globetrotter

"*In Search of a Father's Blessing* is right on mark with what is happening in our culture. Doug Stringer has his finger on the pulse of the current condition of our generation. It's not a message of hopelessness and doom but of hope and restoration. Doug's blend of God's truth and real-life stories makes for compelling reading and introspection."

—*Jay Mincks*
Executive vice president, Insperity

"Doug Stringer is changing the world. From helping the poor and needy to reaching leaders at every level to facilitating and leading regional and national prayer gatherings, he is touching the masses and influencing nations. Doug's influence over my life has made my walk with God, my ministry, and my personal life soar to greater heights. No one is more suited to write a book like this than Doug Stringer. Because of his example there are many spiritual orphans who are now finding hope and purpose for their lives."

—*Mike Rosas*
Chaplain, Houston Rockets
Cofounder with wife, Lidiette, of Love Bought

DOUG STRINGER

IN SEARCH OF A

FATHER'S BLESSING

THE CRY
OF A LOST
GENERATION

WHITAKER
HOUSE

In Search of a Father's Blessing:
The Cry of a Lost Generation
Originally published as *Who's Your Daddy Now?* Updated and revised.

www.dougstringer.com
www.somebodycares.org

ISBN: 978-1-62911-705-8
Printed in the United States of America
© 2016 by Doug Stringer

Whitaker House
1030 Hunt Valley Circle
New Kensington, PA 15068
www.whitakerhouse.com

Library of Congress Cataloging-in-Publication Data

Names: Stringer, Doug, author.
Title: In search of a father's blessing : the cry of a lost generation / by Doug Stringer.
Description: New Kensington, PA : Whitaker House, 2016. | Includes bibliographical references.
Identifiers: LCCN 2016009786 | ISBN 9781629117058 (trade pbk. : alk. paper)
Subjects: LCSH: Church work with families. | Families--Religious aspects—Christianity. | Fatherless families—United States. | Fathers—Religious aspects—Christianity. | Fatherhood—Religious aspects—Christianity.
Classification: LCC BV4438 .S77 2016 | DDC 259/.1—dc23 LC record available at http://lccn.loc.gov/2016009786

1   2   3   4   5   6   7   8   9   10   11   ⨇   23   22   21   20   19   18   17   16

DEDICATION

To Jeanne and Kenny: my younger sister and brother (always "little" sister and brother to me). At the lowest points of my life, thoughts of you both, and a sense of responsibility I felt to be there for you, are what kept me going. Our family had many challenges, but we were still a family nonetheless. Though Dad was your biological father and my stepfather, he saw no distinction between us. Both Mom and Dad were very proud of each of us. I cherish the memories we share of growing up together. I can still remember being nine and then ten years old, when each of you both were born, and the exuberant joy I felt of having a little sister and brother. Yes, I will always remember the cloth diaper days, before disposables were invented.

To Judy: you were always "Daddy's girl" to your father—my biological father—and I know you miss him dearly. I pray that you would come to know you have a heavenly Father who loves you even more and desires to hold that same place in your heart that our father held.

To my mom, my stepfather, and my biological father: who, by the grace of God, are now all with the Lord. Though growing up was not always easy, I cherish and honor the lessons I learned and the relationship we had as we grew to love one another even more through our adversities and challenges. In reality, I have so many fond memories, especially from our times together after we found a common place of healing in Christ.

To those who are my spiritual sons and daughters—Randy, JT, Andrew, Monica, John, Debbie, Bob, Scott, Dale, Julius, Melanie, and so many more—and to all of those who have adopted me as a father in the faith: what a pleasure it is, by God's grace, to walk this walk with you.

To those like myself who do not know how to be good spiritual parents: may God's grace be multiplies unto you as you learn to be fathers and mothers to an emerging generation.

And especially to an entire emerging generation in pursuit of spiritual fathers: may you receive a fresh revelation of your heavenly Father and the destiny He has for each of you.

IN MEMORY OF JUDGE TONY GUILLORY

Judge Tony Guillory was a man of faith, a champion of courage, and a mighty man of God. He considered me one of his spiritual fathers, yet he was also an example of the father's heart to those around him—though he never even knew his own father. He always found time for others and was often giving of his own time to speak to troubled youth.

Even though Tony was a man of stature in the community—working in Houston as an administrative judge for the EEOC (Equal Employment Opportunity Commission)—he was a man of great humility. He had once been assistant attorney general for the state of Texas, but many people didn't even know that because he was always more interested in listening to others than he was in talking himself.

Tony put God first in all things. He took care of his family—his wife Vickie and their son Marquel. He brought wisdom and quiet strength to our board meetings. Even in the courtroom, those he ruled against still respected him because his judgments were just. He was part of our Mighty Men's ministry, a group of men who meet weekly to become better husbands, fathers, and men of God. He was a man who never had an unkind word to say about anyone.

Having walked with a limp for nine years following liver transplant surgery, one of Ton's greatest desires was to run again and to play ball with is Son. Now, he is running once again in his glorified body! He ran ahead of us all, and he taught us how to triumph, even in adversity.

CONTENTS

FOREWORD

The sun shone brightly over the sky, and the smell of newly cut grass filled the air. We all stood at attention as a casket draped in an American flag was led by a military honor guard to the graveside. How befitting for a man who had contributed so much to a movement that called men to a place of decisiveness, strength, consistency, and personal responsibility. He would say, "God has called me to speak with a prophetic voice to the men of this generation that manhood and Christlikeness are synonymous."

Family and friends gathered to honor the memory of a man who touched them so deeply through his life and ministry. Teary-eyed, they each stepped to the podium to share a testimony or offer their condolences to the family. There were two families attending the funeral of Edwin Louis Cole that day. One of them was his blood family, the Coles, and the other was a family of men to whom he had become a spiritual father, filling a void in their lives. I was one of them.

It was my turn to say a few words. It was difficult to hold back the tears because I saw him as a father and would sorely miss him, like many of the other men. I took the podium and began sharing my story, making sure to look at the Cole family and thank them for sharing this man with us. But I also looked around at the men he had fathered outside of his family, and a prophetic realization rested upon me: It was time for those who had been fathered to become fathers. I finished my brief presentation and returned to my seat, feeling that a new season of men's ministry was dawning.

Also, among those spiritual sons fathered by Dr. Cole was Doug Stringer. He took the message to heart. So I am not surprised that, just a few years later, he is releasing this book, titled, appropriately enough, *In Search of a Father's Blessing.* I believe that every man and woman—fathers, mothers, pastors, youth leaders, husbands, wives, sons, daughters—should read this book. Doug not only raises the issue of fatherlessness, which we are all too familiar with, but he also sends out the clarion call to fill this void for others that already has been filled for us. It is a call to take responsibility for another generation looking for fathers to guide, guard, and govern their lives; to direct, protect, and correct; to lead them into true manhood and true womanhood.

These words were written some nineteen hundred years ago, but they still apply today:

> *For though you may have ten thousand teachers in Christ, you do not have many fathers.*   (1 Corinthians 4:15 NCV)

Thank you, Doug, for this work, and congratulations!

—*Rev. A. R. Bernard Sr.*
Founder and senior pastor, Christian Cultural Center,
Brooklyn, New York

INTRODUCTION: THE CRY OF A GENERATION

Late Sunday night, I received an e-mail from L.

There are times when I feel like "Father" is the worst name God could have given Himself. What a stupid idea, for "father" means rejection in my world.

In 1981, I founded a ministry called Somebody Cares as an outreach effort to battle homelessness and a loss of hope in inner city Houston, Texas. Somebody Cares has implemented several citywide strategies that have been multiplied in cities across the nation, including mentoring programs and anti-gang and at-risk youth intervention training. The ministry has become a model that connects needs with resources during natural and human calamities, such as tornadoes and hurricanes in the US, earthquake and tsunami devastation in Japan, Indonesia, and Haiti, as well as the Asian Economic Collapse of 1998.

I had just spoken one morning at a church we had worked with on relief efforts after Hurricanes Katrina and Rita. My message was about God's love and mercy for the fatherless and His desire to adopt them into His own family.

One of my board members was there, along with his sister. He had become addicted to drugs when he was a young man, and his family had asked me to help locate a full-time recovery regimen for him. So I had helped him get into a Teen Challenge program directed by my friend Roger. Today, he runs the family business and heads up one of our Somebody Cares chapters. He has a beautiful family who all love the Lord.

All these years later, his sister's daughter is going through struggles of her own. It was she who sent the e-mail and gave us permission to share what she had written that night, in hopes of helping others:

I am eighteen years old. I feel God pulling on my heart more than I'm comfortable with, so I'm doing what He has told me to do—write to you. This is my story.

Like my uncle, I'm extremely determined. The last two years of my life have been thorny, to say the least. My dad left when I was sixteen, and ever since, I've had a hard time trusting God. To be honest, there are times when I question His authority and even His existence. I live in a small two-bedroom apartment with my mom and thirteen-year-old brother, so the couch is my best friend.

Almost exactly a year ago, I became pregnant. As you may know, I am adopted, as is my brother, and up until then, I'd always been immovably pro-life. But I knew I had other options, and I had an abortion six weeks later. I knew that I was making a huge mistake. I knew that it would destroy my spirit and tear out my heart, but I did it anyway.

After the impact of what I had done hit me, I drank myself into oblivion every night for about a year. I still struggle with alcohol periodically, but I never really got into drugs, mainly because I didn't like them. I know that if I had, I would most likely be on the street at this point.

I could make excuses as to why I had an abortion, but I still have to live with the choice I made. I hate myself for it, and the sound of the vacuum still haunts my dreams to this day.

However, I've just recently gotten to the point where I'm not ashamed of what I did. I don't try to hide it from people anymore. I want them to know so it doesn't happen to them.

There are times when I feel that I've never really been loved by a person who has touched me. There are times when I feel like "Father" is the worst name God could have given Himself. What a stupid idea, for "father" means rejection in my world.

These last two years, I guess I've been looking for something to justify my pain, to explain why all this has happened and why I am so screwed up. I know that you can find redemption only through God and that no one can do it for you, but I usually stay away from people I'm angry with. Honestly, most days, I want to go "Mike Tyson" on God.

Even though I've never met you, I have an enormous amount of respect for you and for what God did through you in my uncle's life.

I want to be who God wants me to be, and who I am today isn't who God wants me to be. I want God to be proud of me. I want my family to be proud of me. I want to be proud of me.

I really appreciate you for taking the time to read my e-mail. I don't mean to dump all my problems on you or anything; I just felt like writing to you was what God was telling me to do. I'd love to hear back from you.

With utmost respect,

L

Divorce, abandonment, rejection, pregnancy, abortion, alcohol, drugs—in one letter, this young woman addressed many of the issues our fatherless generation faces daily, and most can be traced back to a broken connection with a father. L's story echoes the heart-cry of an entire generation that is looking for the affirmation, acceptance, and approval of a father. What too many of them have experienced instead is abandonment and absence.

L said that "father" means rejection in her world, and she speaks for an entire generation. When I replied to the e-mail, I told her that no matter what she was going through or feeling, God the Father was there for her. I praised her for her honesty, because honesty is attractive to God. It's only in that place of vulnerability that He can begin to bring healing. I could tell she really wanted to help others avoid the pain she had experienced, and I gave her hope that God would use her that way.

A few days later, I met with L in my office, and I listened as she spoke openly from her heart. I let her know that God wanted to take what the enemy intended for evil and use it for her good. I told her that God had a special love for those who are adopted. When she left, she had a hopeful heart and a joyful countenance.

She dreams of ministering someday to other young women who have experienced similar pain. In the meantime, she is receiving Christian counseling and reconciling with her family. Most of all, she is learning to accept God as her Father.

What we have today is a double generation of fatherlessness, consisting of a former generation (mine) and an emerging generation that both grew up, for the most part, without fathers. Even those who have or had good fathers still suffer from the widespread effects of fatherlessness in our culture and our world.

But if God has added grace for the fatherless and for the widow, how much more grace will there be for entire fatherless generations? And if we now have a double generation of fatherlessness, I believe we are going to see a double portion of grace poured out on these two generations, who together will emerge as the "Gen-Edge miracle," a generation living on the edge of eternity. These generations will journey together to become a prophetic generation—a generation spoken of by the prophets of old (see Acts 2:17–18)—rising up to prepare people for the coming of the Lord!

Already we can see signs of this preparation. The Sentinel Group, producers of the Transformation video series, tracks lasting and sustained transformation in communities and nations throughout the world. In 1999, only eight cities were experiencing the kind of revival in which every element of culture is touched. As a former Sentinel Group board member, I can report that by 2009, we knew of one thousand cities worldwide—and even some nations—that were at some point on the journey toward transformational revival.

This tells us that God is doing something quickly, and He will not wait on those who sit back and are stagnant in mediocrity and compromise. He's looking for a standard to be raised! We aren't called to be on the defensive; we should be proactively sharing the life of Christ with the next generation. We must be fathers and mothers to those emerging from life's wilderness, leading them to their Abba-Father through the Spirit of adoption found in relationship with His beloved Son Jesus Christ.

In the late 1980s, God began to give me insight into the state of our nation through the problems our ministry encounters daily as they reach out to individuals struggling with drugs, alcohol, abortion, prostitution, apathy, and so forth. He revealed to me the root and source of all these struggles: America is a nation devoid of fathers, both natural fathers and spiritual fathers. We are an orphaned nation with broken and dysfunctional families, a society of individuals in search of their identity. Recognizing this, I began calling the emerging generation the "no-direction generation."

When I published this in my book *The Fatherless Generation: Hope for a Generation in Search of Identity*, I didn't realize it would be even more relevant today than it was in 1995. More than two decades later, as I complete the book you are reading, the church is just now waking up to its need to father and mother an abandoned generation left to its own devices. And this is a worldwide condition, not one limited to our own country.

By the world's view, the emerging generation is merely one scattered in life's barren deserts, but God is calling them into their destinies! He is releasing forerunners to prepare the way for the coming revival.

The prophets of old yearned to see the days in which we live, because the words God spoke through them are being fulfilled now. This time, it's not about one generation passing a baton to the next. God is a multigenerational God. He is simultaneously the God of Abraham, Isaac, and Jacob. He wants to release a multigenerational anointing on all who are willing.

As He unites the wisdom and resources of former generations with the passion and zeal of the emerging generation, we will become a synergistic, unstoppable force advancing the kingdom of God!

At one of our meetings for emerging leaders, my friend Mike, a fellow minister of the gospel at Somebody Cares Humble, in Humble, Texas, echoed the passionate cries of our hearts with his closing prayer:

> There is a sound within this generation. We've heard its rumblings, but we want to hear its full sound. Breathe on our minds, Lord, in areas where we have been wrestling to release this generation. Breathe on our hearts so that we can see this generation come forth, so that we can see revival come to pass. We are sick and tired of only hearing of the revival; we want to see the revolution. Let the revolution begin!

It is a cry of the heart, a corporate cry for a generation walking through the wilderness of life! We are a prophetic generation, a part of the double generation of the fatherless! It's a multigenerational anointing; we call forth other generations, churches, and even nations to come back to the Father!

The late Leonard Ravenhill once wrote to me, "My dearest brother, Doug, let others live on the raw edge or the cutting edge...you and I should live on the edge of eternity."

On the edge of eternity, bringing in the harvest for the final days—that's the Gen-Edge miracle! I can think of no better place to be!

Are you ready and willing to be part of the journey?

PART 1

A DOUBLE GENERATION OF FATHERLESSNESS

1

"WHO'S YOUR DADDY?"

You might recall this phrase from *Remember the Titans*, in which Denzel Washington plays a high-school football coach. In the movie, Coach Boone is approached by one of his players as the team boards a bus to training camp. The disrespectful young man demeans the coach's authority, to which he responds, "Where's your folks, Gary? Your parents—are they here? Where are they?"

Gary points at his mother, standing across the parking lot.

Boone looks at the mother, then back at her son, and says, "Take a good look at her, cause once you get on that bus, you ain't got no mama no more. You got your brothers on the team, and you got your daddy. Now you know who your daddy is, don't you?"

The young man is silent, unsure of how to answer.

"Who your daddy, Gary?"

No answer.

The coach demands, "Who's your daddy?"

"You," the young player finally replies.

One of my spiritual daughters was asked the same question, but in a different context—she was learning how to fly a helicopter. The view and the sights were incredible. "So who's your daddy?" the pilot jokingly asked her, sensing her enthusiasm.

"You are!" she answered.

Who's your daddy? The question is slang for, "Who's in control of things?" "Who's showing you the ropes?" "Who's taking care of you?" Sometimes, it's meant in a derogatory way, implying control and manipulation and even bullying; other times, it's used comically.

The question is a commentary on our times. We are a generation devoid of the intended intimacy of the family unit, and we compensate through using terms that reflect this lack.

Out of the abundance of the heart the mouth speaks.
(Matthew 12:34)

God wants to be the Abba-Father of an entire generation. *Abba* is Aramaic for "father," a word used to express intimacy and endearment. I don't intend to promote a common, casual, or irreverent depiction of God the Father. He is a holy God, and we honor Him and give the glory due His name. Even in His holiness, He loves us so much that He desires that we have the childlike boldness to come to Him as our Daddy, our Papa, in times of need. (See Hebrews 4:16.)

I believe that at the core of every problem we experience as an individual, a generation, and even a nation is disconnection from a father. It's an issue of breach, an issue of broken trust.

I remember when, as a boy, my trust was broken with my own father. My dad was an underwater demolition frogman—today, we would call him a Navy SEAL. We were at the Naval Amphibious Base Coronado in San Diego, California. To be at the Amphibious Base as a young boy was bigger than life. Dad had bought me brand-new fins and a mask, just like the ones the Navy SEALS used. Dad was already in the water, and I walked up to the edge of the pool, so excited that I could hardly contain myself. But suddenly, I realized my dad was drunk and stopped dead in my tracks.

*I believe that at the core of every problem we experience
as an individual, a generation, and even a nation is
disconnection from a father. It's an issue of breach, an
issue of broken trust.*

"Jump on in, Doug," he said. "Come on in, son. Jump in."

I wanted so badly to jump, to be with my dad. He could swim like
a fish, and I wanted to learn, too. But I was frozen with fear. If he really
loved me, why would he have gotten so drunk? Would I be safe with
him? Could I trust him?

I couldn't do it—I couldn't jump. I was afraid that I would drown
because he wasn't in control of his senses. A measure of intimacy with
my dad was severed that day and was never restored. I never learned
how to swim.

At some point, we've all experienced broken trust. When it happens
repeatedly, we unjustly connect the wounds, hurt, and mistrust from
damaged earthly relationships with our heavenly Father. The result
is generations of orphans who don't understand the love of a heavenly
Father because they never had the love of an earthly father. They don't
know how to trust their heavenly Father because they were unable to
trust their earthly fathers.

So now we have a generation of men and women who don't know
how to be good fathers and mothers trying to raise another generation that is also in need. Entire nations of young men and women have
orphaned themselves from the heavenly Father, or have yet to come into
the revelation that God is their Father. Entire religions have forsaken
the Father because they have denied the Son. (See 1 John 2:23.)

We all are looking for identity through what I call the three As:
affirmation, acceptance, and approval. We look for it as individuals,
generations, and nations.

The redemptive plan of God involves pouring out His grace on
this generation and on entire nations, because He is the Father of all

generations and nations! *"Where sin abounded, grace abounded much more"* writes Paul (Romans 5:20). So when the pain of fatherlessness abounds in a generation, how much more does God's grace abound to them! If the issue is widespread fatherlessness, then the redemptive plan of God involves an outpouring of supernatural grace upon a generation that has not received the love, embrace, or affirmation of their earthly fathers. Are you ready to be a part of His multigenerational outpouring of grace?

We all are looking for identity through...affirmation, acceptance, and approval.

John the Baptist cried out, a lone voice in the wilderness, preparing the way for the coming of the Lord (see Isaiah 40:3); but the emerging generation is crying out with a corporate voice, "The Lord is coming! The Lord is coming!" Can you hear the cry?

God is *"a father of the fatherless, a defender of widows,...[and] sets the solitary in families"* (Psalm 68:5–6). God desires to take orphaned people, "dysfunctional" in the worldly vocabulary, and to set them into the family of the body of Christ. God is calling forth a generation wandering in the desert of life. He wants to give them a focus, a destination, and a destiny, to put a cloak on them, and to empower them to do great things in the name of Christ. He wants to transform a fatherless generation into a prophetic generation!

God waits with open arms for His prodigals to return, and He has sent His Son to find the lost. Are you willing to go the extra mile and join Him?

2

CAMELS IN THE WILDERNESS

Once I was invited to minister at a racial reconciliation meeting in Louisiana, along with another pastor, Levy Knox. During the meeting, Bishop Knox delivered a powerful message on reconciliation titled "The Camels Are Coming," encouraging us to accept and serve whatever camels came our way. Pastor Knox spoke on the account in Genesis 24, when Abraham sent a servant to search for a bride for his son Isaac. The servant took ten camels with him on the journey, which bore not only basic necessities for desert travel but also gifts for the bride.

How will I know when I have found the one meant to be Isaac's bride? the servant wondered. As he pondered, he asked God that the woman would be made known by her willingness to serve her master and anyone in need. The servant found such a woman in Rebecca. She was drawing water at the well and offered some to him and the ten camels that had just journeyed through the desert.

These camels were not only thirsty—they were also dirty, hungry, and smelly. I've been told that one camel can drink up to forty gallons of water after completing a desert journey. That means that this woman was willing to serve those ten thirsty camels up to four hundred gallons of water—and she did so! As she served the camels, she didn't realize that they were bearing gifts on their backs that she would soon receive. She wasn't looking for the gifts; she simply desired to serve.

WHO ARE THE CAMELS?

Pastor Knox's message so resonated with me that I soon began to apply it to my ministry with the emerging generation. So what does this Bible story about a bride and ten camels have to do with a book on spiritual fathers and a generation of orphans? The fact that we can apply it to this subject reveals the beauty of God's Word and all the hidden treasures that lie within it!

We can compare Abraham to the heavenly Father, Abraham's servant to the Holy Spirit, and Isaac to Jesus. Today, the heavenly Father has sent out His Holy Spirit in search of a bride for His Son, a bride who is prepared to serve Him and to serve those in need.

And the camels? We are camels who have come out of the wilderness and have been redeemed. We were dirty, smelly, and thirsty, but someone served us. Jesus filled us with His rivers of living water that never run dry, rivers flowing from the throne of God with healing. And He didn't stop there. God quenched our thirst and began to change our lives, and this cycle continues as our lives are changed through Christ. As we grow up in Him and represent Him as His church and bride, God bids us to reach out and offer others this same Water of Life.

Many of us have lived with immoral lifestyles and addictive behaviors, and we searched constantly for ways to cover our pain. We didn't want to feel the hurt, so we kept running and tried anything we could find to satisfy the longing in our soul.

Many people in this fatherless generation are the same. They are covering up their fears, insecurities, and pain. Now we, as former camels redeemed by God, have an opportunity to be like Rebecca, the servant bride, who was willing to take on the task at hand regardless of the cost.

The book of Revelation presents a picture of the bride preparing herself for Christ:

> [A great multitude said,] *"Let us be glad and rejoice and give Him glory, for the marriage of the Lamb has come, and His wife has made herself ready."* And to her it was granted to be arrayed in fine linen, clean and bright, for the fine linen is the righteous acts of the

saints. Then [the angel] said to me, "Write: 'Blessed are those who
are called to the marriage supper of the Lamb!'" And he said to me,
"These are the true sayings of God."   (Revelation 19:7–9)

As we prepare ourselves for the coming of the Lord, we must commit
to living a holy life and seeking God's kingdom first. (See Matthew
6:33.) We must reach out with the love of God to those who are hungry
and thirsty, for as we serve this generation, we are serving our Lord.
(See Matthew 25:40.) Young people today are like those camels coming
out of the wilderness, and God is looking for individuals and churches
who will serve them and give them a drink.

THE PROPHETIC MANTLE

There is even more to this beautiful story of redemption.

John the Baptist came out of the wilderness dressed in camel's hair,
wearing a leather belt around his waist, and eating locusts and wild
honey. He was extreme, radical, passionate, and full of zeal. Wearing
the camel-hair cloak, he represents the camels—the generation emerging from the wilderness.

In those days John the Baptist came preaching in the wilderness of
Judea, and saying, "Repent, for the kingdom of heaven is at hand!"
For this is he who was spoken of by the prophet Isaiah, saying: "The
voice of one crying in the wilderness: 'Prepare the way of the LORD;
make His paths straight.'" Now John himself was clothed in camel's
hair, with a leather belt around his waist; and his food was locusts
and wild honey.   (Matthew 3:1–4)

The cloak of camel's hair is symbolic of a prophetic covering. Today,
the church is to go forth with the spirit of John the Baptist, proclaiming
the coming of the Lord, liberty to the captives, and healing to the bro-
kenhearted. (See Isaiah 61:1.) This emerging generation of redeemed
orphans are each called to be a modern-day John the Baptist. Like their
predecessor, they are to be extreme, radical, passionate, and full of zeal.
God is clothing them with a prophetic mantle, equipping them to do

the work He has ordained for them from the very foundations of the world. (See Ephesians 2:10.)

In preparation for the Lord's return, the hearts of many in this generation will turn back not only to their earthly father but to their heavenly Father, as well. God is already pouring out His grace upon this generation, which so desperately needs Him. Scripture says,

> *And it shall come to pass afterward that I will pour out My Spirit on all flesh; your sons and your daughters shall prophesy, your old men shall dream dreams, your young men shall see visions. And also on My menservants and on My maidservants I will pour out My Spirit in those days.* (Joel 2:28–29)

God spoke of those who will live an uncompromising life for Him and boldly proclaim His truth and mercy to spiritually nomadic people wandering in the wilderness. From this very generation of wandering drifters will come prophets and prophetesses, who, transformed by the power of God, will proclaim and prepare the way for the coming of the Lord.

Many of the camels in the wilderness are desperate for change, and they are looking for someone to guide them. When they come to know the living God, they are radical! They aren't ashamed of the gospel of Jesus Christ, for it is the power of God unto salvation.

> *For I am not ashamed of the gospel of Christ, for it is the power of God to salvation for everyone who believes.* (Romans 1:16)

This generation knows the road of heartache and the pathway of pain; but when they come to Christ, they're ready for sweeping change. Then from that place of brokenness and gratitude, they go out boldly, proclaiming truth and rescuing others.

3

A GENERATION
IN NEED

In 2002, there were 52 million Americans who had been born between 1922 and 1945. They are called the Veteran/Traditionalist Generation. The baby boomers were born between 1945 and 1960, and were followed by the Xers, born between the 1960s and 1970s. Generation X had the greatest lack of fathers. In algebra, "x" stands for the unknown quotient. Society gave Gen Xers this label, implying that they are wandering drifters.

An online source reads,

> Generation X has survived a hurried childhood of divorce, latchkeys, space shuttle explosions, open classrooms, widespread public knowledge of political corruption, inflation and recession, post-Vietnam national malaise, environmental disaster, the Islamic Revolution (in Iran), devil-child movies, and a shift from "G" to "R" ratings....
>
> Divorce became commonplace and affected families of all social and economic backgrounds. Naturally, Gen Xers were affected by the continual bombardment of TV images of the nuclear family (*Brady Bunch, Happy Days*) in contrast to their own; and feelings of inadequacy and isolation from society resulted."[1]

---

1. "X – The Next Generation," Baby Boomer Central, http://www.babyboomercentral. com.au/next.htm.

The current generation of young people born after 1980, known as Millennials or Generation Y, have inherited the fruit of previous generations, as we can see in the following statistics:

+ One-third has been drunk in the last month.

+ One in four uses illegal drugs.

+ 8,000 contract a sexually transmitted disease (STD) every day.

+ One million Gen Ys are pregnant, and 340,000 get abortions every year.

+ One in ten has been raped.

+ They will see 14,000 sexual references on TV this year, and nine out of ten of them have seen pornography online.

+ Half of the Millennials are no longer virgins.

+ 40 percent have inflicted self-injury.

+ One in five has contemplated suicide, and over 1,500 actually kill themselves every year.[2]

Gen Ys are not only fatherless, many of them are angry and confused, and lack direction. They have been hurt and react accordingly, but they act as if they don't care. And Satan is determined to rob them of their destinies.

The media blitz constantly tells them that they don't measure up. They are bombarded with sin meant to desensitize them. Our young people, even those who try to fight against it, are faced with immeasurable challenges. Sadly, too many of them face these challenges alone.

Furthermore, when Christians try to preach the gospel about our Father God, the younger generation often responds with cynicism. They have no comprehension of a heavenly Father because they have no comprehension of an earthly father.

---

2. Adapted from list in Ron Luce, *Battle Cry for a Generation: The Fight to Save America's Youth* (Colorado Springs, CO: David C. Cook, 2005).

A CRISIS OF IDENTITY

In my book *Hope for a Fatherless Generation*, I pointed out that 50–60 percent of our young people grow up in single-parent homes, and the majority of them don't have relationships with their father—even if they know who he is.[3]

While teaching at an urban camp of two hundred fifty inner-city kids, I asked if any had a healthy relationship with their father. The majority of them tearfully said that they didn't. I serve as an advisor of a home for runaway boys and troubled youth, which asks all the applicants this same question. One time, out of the six hundred twenty boys who had been interviewed, less than twenty of them claimed to have a healthy relationship with their father.

In his "Father Knows Best" broadcast series, Pastor Jack Graham of PowerPoint Ministries said that the average American father spends eight minutes a day with his children.[4] According to the National Fatherhood Initiative, 24 million children in the United States live in homes without fathers,[5] and, in 2002, 20 million lived in single-parent homes.[6] Furthermore, 40 percent of children in father-absent homes have not even seen their dads within the past year; 50 percent have never set foot in their father's home; and 26 percent of absent fathers don't even live in the same state as their children.[7]

How sad for a nation that once took pride in not only knowing the heavenly Father but also the strength of its families, especially its fathers. Many fathers today are having an identity crisis, which results in women with identity crises, trying to be both mother *and* father. This leads to children who grow up with identity crises, confused about their genders and roles within their own families.

---

3. Doug Stringer, *Hope for a Fatherless Generation* (Shippensburg, PA: Destiny Image Publishers, Inc., 1995, 2009).

4. Jack Graham, "Father Knows Best," PowerPoint Ministries, podcast audio, June 2007.

5. "Statistics on the Father Absence Crisis in the United States," The National Fatherhood Initiative, http://www.fatherhood.org/father-absence-statistics.

6. "Single-parent Families," Encyclopedia of Children's Health, http://www. healthofchildren.com/S/Single-Parent-Families.html.

7. Tom Davis and Tammy Maltby, *Confessions of a Good Christian Guy: The Secrets Men Keep and the Grace That Saves Them* (Nashville, TN: Thomas Nelson, 2006).

The book *Rachel's Tears: The Spiritual Journey of Columbine Martyr Rachel Scott* chronicles the life of a student who died for her faith in the Columbine High School shootings in 1999. Much of the book consists of her own journal writings as well as observations from her parents.

Rachel's father and mother separated when she was seven years old and later divorced. After Rachel's tragic and premature death, her parents read her journal entries and discovered how she had felt torn between her parents with conflicting loyalties and feelings of abandonment. The immensity of their daughter's pain came as a surprise because they knew her faith in God and bold witness were so strong. They'd known that the divorce would be hard on all their children, so they'd wisely committed to never speak ill of each another. They loved their daughter immensely and did everything they could to ease her pain, but it was still a struggle.

Her father, Darrell Scott, wrote, "Regardless of the reasons for a divorce, it is never easy when children are involved. Children will always be affected by divorce."[8]

Our heavenly Father revealed His perfect plan for every family at the dawn of creation, which was, and still is, one man and one woman raising a family together. He never intended that a child should have to choose between his or her mom and dad. He never intended for the woman to be both mother and father. The spiritual, mental, and emotional atrophy pulling at men, women, and children today was not His design.

So what do we do as a church in the context of this reality? How do we get back to a place where the Lord is the nucleus of our families, our generations, and our nation? We must turn our focus back to God the Father.

God desires to strengthen men so that they can guide, guard, and govern their homes with the love of Christ. When this happens, there will be security in the home. However, above all, God's greatest desire is to be our Father and to bring us into His family through the Spirit of adoption.

8. Darrell Scott and Beth Nimmo, *Rachel's Tears: The Spiritual Journey of Columbine Martyr Rachel Scott*, 10th Anniversary Edition, (Nashville, TN: Thomas Nelson, 2000, 2008), 55.

A GENERATION LOST

Throughout history, Satan's plan has been to kill men and their destinies while they are yet in their infancy. (See John 10:10.) Pharaoh slew the infants in Egypt trying to kill Moses. Herod murdered all male infants in Bethlehem in hopes of killing Jesus. Now, Satan is targeting our youth and children at their most vulnerable age to keep them from entering into their God-ordained destinies.

Satan knows that this generation is set apart by God for mighty exploits, in spite of the grim statistics and what looks hopeless to the natural eye. The destroyer knows that his time is short, and he is doing everything possible to postpone the inevitable by distracting this generation and thus keeping it from fulfilling its true destiny in Christ Jesus.

From September 2000 to November 2003, I had the pleasure of serving with The Call, an organization that sponsors youth meetings of prayer, fasting, repentance, and sacrificial worship. During a series of youth gatherings, birthed from the vision of Lou Engle and Ché Ahn, I saw multigenerational members of the body of Christ come together to empower the emerging generation. More than one million young people gathered in seven locations across America, beginning in Washington, DC, and ending in the Cotton Bowl in Dallas, Texas. Each event consisted of an entire day of prayer, fasting, and worship, from sunup to sundown. There were no performances, no personal agendas, only a multigenerational outcry of praise, worship, and passionate prayers for God to touch the emerging generation!

Satan knows that his time is short, and he is doing everything possible to postpone the inevitable by distracting this generation and thus keeping it from fulfilling its true destiny in Christ Jesus.

The reason we chose Dallas to host The Call Texas was because we believed it played a major role in birthing the "death culture." It was in Dallas where abortion was made legal in 1973 with the passing of *Roe v.*

Wade, unleashing a travesty of death across the nation. Since that time, almost 58 million lives have been taken before they had ever taken a first breath.[9]

Do you comprehend the significance of that number, the stark reality of it all? Over 58 million lives! No matter what a person believes about abortion, it is absolutely tragic that an entire generation of lives have been sacrificed on the altar of irresponsibility and convenience in this modern-day holocaust, which is readily accepted and even defended by society and blessed by lawmakers. But children of God, rest assured,

> *God will wipe away every tear from their eyes; there shall be no more death, nor sorrow, nor crying. There shall be no more pain, for the former things have passed away.*   (Revelation 21:4)

At The Call Dallas, I spoke this Scripture over these generations, declaring,

> There shall be no more death. It's time to take off our grave-clothes! It's time to take off the things that are binding us and hindering us from walking in the fullness of all that God has for us. It's time to come forth!

KIDS WHO CARE

Tim Clinton, president of the American Association of Christian Counselors, wrote in one of his letters to his colleagues:

> In a nation that claims to be very dedicated to kids, shamefully they are our most underserved population. And with the exception of those adults who really care about children, they have no advocate. I love the quote from Fran Stott, "Every child needs at least one person who is crazy about [him]."[10]

---

9. Steven Ertlet, "57,762,169 Abortions in America Since *Roe vs. Wade* in 1973," LifeNews.com, January 21, 2015, http://www.lifenews.com/2015/01/21/57762169-abortions-in-america-since-roe-vs-wade-in-1973/.

10. Tim Clinton, "Caring for Kids God's Way," http://timclinton.com/store/courses/2/caring-kids-gods-way/.

The enemy wants our children to believe that there is no one who cares about them. He wants us all to believe that an unborn life is not a life at all. But even as Satan ruthlessly attacks, God's Spirit is moving just as mightily among children in many areas throughout the world.

George and Pam, our missionaries to Southeast Asia, began a children's prayer initiative in one of the countries where they served and shared that the prayer ministry is now actually led by a young woman who learned how to pray through her involvement with the ministry, and who took over the leadership at age fifteen. Other friends of ours have shared reports of children in India, Indonesia, and other locations who are moving in prophetic and healing gifts. We also see God raising up children who are expressing His heart through compassion for the hurting. We call them "Kids Who Care."

Originally from Iran, Katia and her family are now my neighbors in Houston, and they are also brothers and sisters in the Lord. One Christmas, things were tough for their family, and the father was working two jobs. One was part-time at a local fast food restaurant where I stop for my morning coffee. One day, while in the middle of our Holiday of Hope program, collecting food and toys and distributing funds to thousands of families throughout the city, I stopped at the food chain for coffee. After visiting Katia's father, I decided that I wanted to do something special for the family during the holidays.

Meanwhile, unbeknownst to me, God had touched Katia's heart to help serve the children of the city around Christmastime through Somebody Cares. She set up a table at her church one Sunday to sell her own hand-drawn pictures. Before her family received a gift from Somebody Cares, she came to my house to present a small ceramic Christmas container filled with coins to donate to the work of our ministry.

I was overwhelmed by this little girl's ability to see past her own needs and her compassion for others. I thought of the story of David when his mighty men broke through the armies of the Philistines to bring him a drink from the well of Bethlehem. (See 2 Samuel 23:15–17; 1 Chronicles 11:17–19.) Like David, I felt unworthy to receive Katia's precious gift. It still sits on my bookshelf as a reminder of this one child's heart of compassion and generosity.

K. J. is another one of our kids who care. He was only five years old when he saw news stories of families who lost everything in Hurricane Katrina. Immediately, he began packing up his own toys to send to them. This small act of compassion led to a campaign throughout the city of Omaha, Nebraska, which resulted in a truckload of toys arriving at our offices in Houston to distribute to hurricane evacuees during Christmastime. He and his mother even flew here to help give them away.

Alyson had heard about our ministry with hurricane evacuees through her church in York, Pennsylvania, which we partner with. On her tenth birthday, she asked her friends to not bring gifts to her birthday party but money for hurricane relief instead. They sent us $220.

Amanda was ten years old when she visited New Orleans with her parents during a Somebody Cares hurricane relief outreach. And she was so moved at the immense loss and destruction caused by Hurricane Katrina that she went throughout her neighborhood doing face painting to raise money for the children in New Orleans.

A WAKE-UP CALL

We called the last Call event "The Wake-Up Call," recognizing that if we neglect this great responsibility to become fathers to this generation, we will lose them to the wiles of the enemy.

When speaking at Rock City Church in Baltimore, Maryland, the late Fuchsia Pickett delivered a message about the great move of the Holy Spirit from the early 1900s, which brought about a great restoration of the Spirit's work in churches everywhere. Then, in the late 1960s and early 1970s, the Jesus Movement emerged.

Because the Trinity includes three persons, she said, the next great move throughout the land would focus on the father heart of God, beginning with "the hearts of the fathers turning to the children and the hearts of the children turning to their fathers." (See Malachi 4:6.) Significantly, the first Call rally focused on this theme, beginning the revolutionary release of the father heart of God not only within the church but through whole communities. More than 425,000 people attended this rally, which was held on The Mall in Washington, DC, in September 2000.

Participating in movements like The Call, Generation Joshua, Chain Reaction, and others, I've realized that there has been a groundswell of youth from this wandering generation calling out, "We want to connect to something." They are not satisfied with the status quo; they are crying out to God, "We want the blessing of the Father! We want the covering of our parents and our spiritual parents! We want to be released into our uniqueness!"

The present generation is looking for the embrace and affirmation of a father, and when they come to the revelation of their heavenly Father, there's a radical response—they're willing to do whatever it takes to be that prophetic generation.

God has been giving wake-up calls to us all. We've experienced challenges around the world—global uncertainties and shifting, an increase in natural disasters, and wars and rumors of wars. (See Matthew 24:6.) Yet, in the midst of it all, God is raising up a multigenerational army to honor Him, honor one another, and release this emerging generation into its destiny.

It's been a wake-up call, and many of us have been pushing our snooze buttons. But now it's time to respond to the call. The clarion call from God for this generation is to rise up and fulfill the words spoken over it in Scripture.

God is raising up a multigenerational army to honor Him, honor one another, and release this emerging generation into its destiny.

Could it be that we will see the culmination of all the words spoken by the prophets of old in this generation? Is it possible that this generation is starting to fulfill its destiny to prepare the way for the coming of the Lord?

A PROPHETIC CULMINATION

Statistics paint a grim picture of the future, leaving little room for hope. Nonetheless, God is still in charge, and many from this emerging generation have already come forth despite the barrage of attacks coming against them. And when they do choose to stand for God, they are full of zeal and a passionate desire to do great things for the Lord.

God wants to transform the misfit Generation X into Generation Excellent, a generation of expectancy for the coming revival. He wants to use Generation Y to lead His people into the Promised Land. They are not just the Joshuas, John the Baptists, Elishas, and Elijahs of today; they are a culmination of all that anointing, a prophetic generation God has brought together for this season!

Past generations are crucial to this plan, because God is calling men and women to parent, guide, bless, and release the youth to do mighty exploits for Him. If the bride does not do her part in obeying Christ's mandate to come alongside and empower the young, the devil will continue to destroy the very ones God wants to raise up. He will continue his onslaught of God's people through abortions, gangs, murder, and suicide.

Past generations are crucial to this plan, because God is calling men and women to parent, guide, bless, and release the youth to do mighty exploits for Him.

Satan is trying to rob this generation's identities and destinies, but they are not lost yet. They need direction to find their way out of the wilderness, and we who have gone before them are the ones who can show them.

Will we be like Rachel, who wept over the bloodshed of a generation, or will we be like Elizabeth, who rejoiced over the release of her generation's forerunner? The responsibility is up to us. May God's purpose prevail!

4

A NATION
OF ORPHANS

There is an identity crisis in America, but it is not limited to the emerging generation.

Our society is one in which liberal educators are rewriting textbooks and even denying the existence of the faith of our founding fathers. We are fatherless and orphaned in a historical sense, a spiritual sense, and a practical sense.

We are witnessing the "de-Christ-ing" of our nation. The only One who is pure of heart and pure of purpose, who is liberator and justice-giver, is Jesus Christ. When we take Him out of the equation, there is no liberty, salvation, deliverance, or healing, because these cannot not exist on earth without Him. And to take away the spiritual and moral values from a people is to leave them to journey toward anarchy, because to deny the Son is also to deny the Father. (See 1 John 2:23.)

A NATION OF ORPHANS
Many people have denied authority, especially God's authority. Those who stand for righteousness are mocked. It seems as if Americans are shouting, "We don't want God!"—except, of course, when they want His blessings. This is much like a teenager who wants nothing do with his parents and denies their authority until he wants the keys to the car.

We want God on our terms, not His. He becomes whoever or whatever we want Him to be. We often try to recreate God in our own image, forgetting that He made us in His own image.

Just as children without a father's teaching and discipline follow a path of rebellion and lawlessness, so a nation whose people neglect their God-given responsibilities to be what God has preordained also follow a path of rebellion and lawlessness. Without heeding the direction and discipline of our heavenly Father in society, we will continue to see a rise in violence, immorality, and lawlessness in our communities. These are realities we must face. They are the inevitable consequences of fatherlessness!

Just as children without a father's teaching and discipline follow a path of rebellion and lawlessness, so a nation whose people neglect their God-given responsibilities to be what God has preordained follow a path of rebellion and lawlessness.

God ordained America to be a nation that would honor Him, but we have turned our backs on Him. We have orphaned ourselves not only from God the heavenly Father but from our founding fathers by denying the One for whom they gave their lives and upon whose principles they established the laws of the land. And now we are reaping the results.

Blessed is the nation whose God is the LORD.   (Psalm 33:12)

FAULTY FOUNDATIONS

My friend Curt from Youth-Reach Houston was in the Gulf Coast area immediately after Hurricane Ivan hit in 2004. He saw the destruction and devastation left in Ivan's path—not only shattered dwellings but broken lives and dreams. I witnessed the same thing when I visited New Orleans and the Gulf Coast areas of Mississippi after the tragic destruction of Hurricane Katrina in 2005.

Just as the houses built on sand could not withstand Hurricanes Ivan and Katrina, so we will not withstand the shaking that is coming without the foundation of Jesus. As long as our nation sits on a cracked and unstable foundation, we will not be able to survive the storms of life.

This is where many Americans are today. Just as a family without a father is shaky, vulnerable, and out of balance, so, too, are we as a nation. We are like a house built on sand, with a cracked and very faulty foundation. And though it may appear to the outside world and even to ourselves that our foundation is intact, when the storms of life come— be they economic, spiritual, or natural disasters—our house is going to crumble. (See Matthew 7:24–27.)

A VISION OF HOPE

Prior to a presidential election, I was invited to deliver the invocation at one of the largest state gatherings of any political party. There were more than 17,000 people in attendance. The Lord put it on my heart to present the need for a revival of character from the pulpits all the way to the White House. I shared how a great leader named Solomon once said, "*Hope deferred makes the heart sick*" (Proverbs 13:12). Then I quoted the great King Hezekiah, who once said, in a day of trouble and distress, "The children are ready to come to birth, but there is no strength to deliver them." (See 2 Kings 19:3.)

I said that we live in the same kind of predicament. We have a whole generation of young people either sacrificed before they are born or born without a vision of hope or purpose.

We need to give such a vision again—a vision of hope, a vision of purpose, a vision of destination. (See Proverbs 29:18.) We cannot do this through institutional Christianity, shallow platitudes, or business as usual. We can cast vision only by returning to Jesus as our first love, being lovesick for His presence, and once again embracing our heavenly Father as Lord of our hearts and Lord of our land. Human wisdom and man-made efforts have failed us. As Scripture says, "*Unless the LORD builds the house, they labor in vain who build it*" (Psalm 127:1).

REDEEMING OUR MISTAKES

As we've seen, the baby boomers have been tagged as a greedy generation. They constituted the hippie era and were also regarded as the Me generation. As their radicalism was tempered, the boomers became the Yuppies. These upwardly mobile young adults enjoyed success and prosperity, but morally they fell short.

In 1973, after the *Roe v. Wade* Supreme Court decision, they became the generation that aborted its babies under state sanctions, enabling them to abdicate responsibility for their actions. Indeed, there seemed to be no consequences for their actions; doing their own thing was never easier.

Fast-forward to the following generation, which paid dearly for the errors of those who went before. Many lack spirituality and identity, and a large percentage of them grew up in homes with absent fathers. In the wake of their selfish living, the boomers left a generation in an identity crisis. According to an article in the airlines magazine *Continental*, 3 million of the 78 million baby boomers turned sixty in 2001. It went on to say, "[They] want more spiritual enrichment in retirement along with simplicity, and they are willing to downsize to get it."[11] They have tried what the world has to offer but have found it lacking. Bradley Creed, Samford University professor of religion, said, "Baby boomers are deeply concerned with self-actualization and spiritual growth."[12]

God gives grace, and we can learn from the mistakes and errors of the past generations. Even through their failures, many baby boomers have found the wisdom of God and their value in the dreams God has given them, even those yet to be realized. After years of frustration and searching, those who've found the Lord Jesus Christ and have a relationship with the heavenly Father now have wisdom to share with the next generation.

Jeremy from the youth outreach program Generation Xcel understands this well. At our ministry's think tank for emerging leaders in 2004, he said, "As an emerging generation, it is very important that we

---

11. "From Boomers to Zoomers," *Continental*, June 2001, 26.
12. Bradley Creed, *New Choices*, November 2001.

recognize we would not be able to do anything without the men and women of the generation who have gone before us and are leading us through their wisdom. We must honor them. We don't want a generation who hands us the checkbook and leaves us. We need our spiritual fathers!"

After years of frustration and searching, those who've found the Lord Jesus Christ and have a relationship with the heavenly Father now have wisdom to share with the next generation.

The current younger generation has great passion, zeal, and vision. As they become sanctified and released into their destinies, they need the covering, wisdom, and strength of the previous generations. They do not need wisdom that quenches their zeal and passion; they need true wisdom, which empowers, strengthens, encourages, and releases them into their destinies. Then we will see the dreams of the older accomplished through the vision and passion of the younger.

BRIDGING THE GAP

I am part of what I call the "cusp" generation, the group at the tail end of the hippie movement and at the beginning of the yuppie movement. Though I was too young to join the hippie movement, I experienced the outcomes—the walk-outs from school, long hair, LSD, marijuana—the legacies of the Me generation. We were not responsible for prohibiting officially sponsored prayers in public schools, but we were given the responsibility of the fallout.

My age group was stuck between two generations. I was not in the group who laid the foundation for these things; I was simply a by-product of it. I have one foot in the "turn on, tune in, drop out" generation, to borrow the phrase coined by Timothy Leary in the 1960s. Yet my other foot is in a different generation of crisis, the one consumed with trying to find success—the yuppie generation.

This generation looks to accomplish greatness by fulfilling personal needs at the expense of others. As Dr. Cole used to say, "Love desires to give at the expense of self, but lust desires to get at the expense of others."

But God can use those of us who are stuck in the middle. We have learned much from having one foot in one generation and one foot in another. We can be the bridge that connects those who have gone before us with those who will come after us. Because we are able to relate to both generations, we can become a bridge-building, peacemaking, ambassadorial people. We can link the older generation with its wisdom and dreams to the younger generation with its vision and passion.

A 2001 *U.S. News & World Report* article reported, "Demographers anticipate the boomer generation will rewrite what it means to be a senior citizen. They'll take tai chi classes in their 90s, start second careers at 60, and begin romances at ages that will bring frowns to the foreheads of their grandkids."[13]

Aging boomers are Rollerblading, skydiving, and looking for activities to keep them in touch with their youth. Yet the very things boomers are looking for are the things the X and Y generations already have! The older generations are trying to live on the edge, and the younger ones already are. The generation gap is not as big as some may think.

Yet it does exist. Not only have the baby boomers generally failed to appreciate and honor the prior generations, they have also viewed the younger generations with contempt. The boomers have pasted derogatory labels on the younger generations, such as "lazy," "unmotivated," and "good-for-nothing." Instead getting to know them, we often stand at a distance and shake our heads with scorn, asking, "Can anything good come from this generation?"

But this is not God's intention. God is multigenerational, and He wants to bridge the generation gaps. He desires unity among all age groups to fulfill His plan upon the earth.

"God wants to take the wisdom of the old generation, the resources of the middle generation, and the zeal of the young generation to bring

---

13. Tim Smart and James M. Pethokoukis, "Not Acting Their Age," *U.S. News & World Report*, 130, no. 22 June 2001, 56.

revival," said Mark from Blood-N-Fire Ministries San Antonio, one of our Somebody Cares affiliates.

The enemy, he says, uses two things to stop revolution. "First, we despise the old, which means we lose the opportunity to glean from their wisdom. Then, we look at the young generation and despise them as they are inventing and creating. If we can maintain unity in the midst of diversity, we can maintain the synergism necessary!"

When God called Jeremiah into his prophetic ministry, Jeremiah responded,

> *"Ah, Lord GOD! Behold, I cannot speak, for I am a youth." But the LORD said to* [him]: *"Do not say, 'I am a youth,' for you shall go to all to whom I send you, and whatever I command you, you shall speak."*   (Jeremiah 1:6–7)

Age is irrelevant to God. He doesn't want the generations to be separated. It is time for restoration and the realization that we need each other. As we cross racial and denominational lines to become part of something bigger than ourselves, so we must cross generational lines.

Then we will link together to fulfill God's purposes for all generations. God is calling us to realize a destiny none of us can accomplish alone. With the dreams and wisdom of the older generation and the vision, passion, and zeal of the younger generation, we all can live on the edge for Christ. We can be part of the Gen-Edge miracle!

Each generation is looking to live on that cutting edge. We all are trying to fill the longing of our hearts and souls. And in Christ, the yearnings of every generation will be fulfilled. Living on the edge of eternity for Christ is the greatest extreme sport, the greatest experience we could ever have!

WHAT'S IN IT FOR ME?

Drugs, alcohol, and gangs are not the real problem of any given generation; they are by-products of a deeper dilemma. Drugs and alcohol provide escape from a world of pain, and gangs provide a sense of family to those who don't have one. External expressions of rebellion are indications of internal hurt.

I attribute many of the problems in America to my own generation—the baby boomers, those who were born post-World War II, from the late 1940s into the early 1960s. I was on the tail end of the "boomer" generation. Our generation is sometimes called the "Me" generation. Our motto was, "If it feels good, do it." And our ethical philosophy was embodied in the statement "I'm not hurting anybody else. It's my life, and I'll do what I want." Character was irrelevant. Commitment was unnecessary.

This lack of character and commitment produced legalized abortion, higher divorce rates, and single-parent homes, in which women had to be both a mother and father to their children. Men abdicated their influence by not behaving in a Christlike way toward women, and women responded with the feminist movement. Many men refused to take responsibility for their actions.

What ought to have been an era of godly liberation and spiritual freedom was characterized by a national identity crisis. What should have brought freedom brought more bondage. Engaging in relationship without commitment led to a chasm not only between genders but between generations, as well.

Unfortunately, this "me" culture even permeated the atmosphere of some our churches, producing Christians who tell themselves, "Whatever makes me feel good is right?" Yes, we need to be relevant in our teaching, but if it does not get past the surface, our disciples will have nothing to stand on when they are hit by the storms of life.

Like the Shulamite with her lover in Song of Solomon, we must be lovesick once again for God. "Revival comes by desperation," said Jackson Senyonga of Uganda, "and desperation comes one of two ways: passion or persecution." The late Leonard Ravenhill understood the same principle. "God doesn't answer prayer," he said, "He answers desperate prayer!" And I would add to that, "God answers desperate and passionate prayer."[14]

---

14. Doug Stringer, "Pray Until Something Happens," *Charisma & Christian Life*, magazine 24, no. 8, March 1999.

Our passion for God allows no room for mediocrity or compromise. God is not looking for shallow platitudes or religious incantations. He does not desire a surface relationship, in which His children interact with Him only when they want something. God desires intimacy and conversation with His creation.

Our passion for God allows no room for mediocrity or compromise. God is not looking for shallow platitudes or religious incantations....He desires intimacy and conversation with His creation.

God our Father does not want to be seen as a sugar daddy in the sky. He wants a relationship with His children. Just as a child needs affirmation from his father, so a father needs to be honored and respected by his children. Blessings flow as the result of this intimate engagement. So don't seek the blessing; seek the Father.

MUDDY RELIGION

We live in a nation of muddy religion—a place where new age philosophy mingles with Buddhism; where atheism, Hinduism, and Christianity are all tossed together in a "religion stew." It is no wonder our youth have little concept of absolute truth. Jeffery L. Sheler wrote in *U.S. News & World Report*, "Nationwide, there are now more Buddhists than Presbyterians and nearly as many Muslims as Jews."[15]

"Many Americans seek spiritual sustenance beyond organized religion, in personal experiences and meditative practices. More than four out of five Americans say they have 'experienced God's presence or a spiritual force' close to them, and 46 percent say it has happened many times. 'People are reaching out in all directions in their attempt to escape from the seen world to the unseen world,' explains pollster George Gallup Jr. 'There is a deep desire for spiritual moorings—a hunger for God.'"[16]

15. Jeffery L. Sheler, "Faith in America," *U.S. News & World Report*, May 6, 2002.
16. Ibid.

The bottom line is this: Hunger is there. The world is searching for what popular culture terms "spirituality," and people will continue to find it in alternative ways if we do not point the way to the one true answer.

A MATTER OF FAMILY

God is unleashing a multigenerational anointing, but the enemy is unleashing a multigenerational attack. It's not only an assault on the biological family but also on the spiritual family—the church—and it's a battle we must fight first and foremost on our knees. It's a battle we fight by drawing closer to, growing in intimacy with, the One who gives us liberty and life.

We cannot take lightly our responsibility to be a beacon of truth to the upcoming generations and to the world. My spiritual father Dr. Cole used to say, "You cannot compensate through sacrifice what you lose through disobedience."

Those who live outside our borders will tell us that if the American church ever falls, so will the lives and liberties of those who dwell in other nations across the globe. Our very futures hang in the balance, as do the destinies of our families, the emerging generation, and our nation. Our churches are sick and orphaned because they have forsaken their Father. They have left their first love.

But Jesus Christ remains our Savior, Healer, Deliverer, and Liberator. There is nothing too difficult for Him when He is truly on the thrones of our hearts and on the thrones of the pulpits in America. We can't fix things in our own strength, but if we make ourselves available, God can use us to reach the generations for Him. He can heal us and seal us, through the Spirit of adoption, so we can be fathers and mothers to those coming after us. The curses of past generations will be broken when we allow God to work through our churches to change the present generation!

God is challenging us to live a life of excellence and to do all that we do unto Him—serving one another, the body of Christ, and the lost.

If we do this, the world, our nation, and the emerging generation will see the love of Christ and be drawn to the Father. Why? Because they hunger for genuine truth. People must see something different about us so that they are drawn to our genuineness. Scripture says,

> *Let your light so shine before men, that they may see your good works and glorify your Father in heaven.*　　(Matthew 5:16)

God wants us to take off our lampshades so His light and life can shine through us and draw all men—from all nations and all generations—unto Him.

PART 2

THE ROLES
OF MOMMIES AND
DADDIES

5

LEADING BY EXAMPLE

Mommy, where do daddies come from?" In some cases, this hard question supplants the awkward query "Where do babies come from?" Mothers are sometimes stumped in their efforts to explain where daddies come from, especially when the father is absent in a child's life. It seems that fathers, instead of being the cornerstone of the family, have become a rare commodity.

How can the generation who grew up without understanding the love of earthly mothers and fathers, be spiritual mothers and fathers to others? How can they help the emerging generation understand the love of the heavenly Father?

In 1981, we began Somebody Cares by reaching out to the lost on the streets of Houston. The youth we encountered almost always had one thing in common—the absence of a father.

Today, ministries such as Montrose Street Reach, part of our Somebody Cares Houston network of ministries, continues the work we began in the 1980s. At one of their annual fund-raising banquets, some youth who had come to know Jesus shared their testimonies. The common denominator in their pathways to destruction was physical, sexual, or emotional abuse, either directly from their fathers or indirectly through their father's lack of presence and protection in the home.

We have a responsibility to this generation looking for spiritual fathers. We must adopt this orphaned generation and direct them toward our heavenly Father, who desires to seal them with His Spirit of adoption.

Many in my generation simply don't know how to be good fathers, including me. But those who are desperate for fathers are not expecting us to know how to father but just to be willing. Willingness brings a release of God's grace, which enables us.

LEARNING TO LEAD

In spring 2004, I hosted a think tank for emerging leaders of the emerging generation. What started as a small gathering escalated into more than sixty leaders from across the country, including youth workers, college ministry leaders, worship leaders, seasoned pastors, marketplace ministers, ministry networkers, intercessors, and others. As each of them spoke, I realized that the recurring theme was the need for spiritual fathers. I already knew that the younger generation was looking for spiritual fathers—that's why I invited those who are serving on the front lines to participate in "out of the box" ministries—what surprised me, however, was the leaders' need for spiritual fathers!

When we older men said that we didn't know how to be good fathers because we were fatherless, too, they responded, "We're not asking you to know how, and we're not asking you to be perfect. We're not even asking you to give us anything. But would you journey with us? We want to know that there's someone who has gone before us, someone who can be there for us, just to give us advice. We want to know that we can call you. We want to know that you're praying for us. We don't need a lot of time; we just need to know we can connect."

Just like the generation they are leading, the leaders are looking for connection and covering. One young minister, who considers me a spiritual father, said, "I was saved and raised in church, but then I backslid, recommitted, and struggled for many years because I didn't have a spiritual father." As a result, his ministry is now centered on spiritual fathering. "If it isn't relational," he says, "we don't do it."

Pastor Mike of Freedom International Church in Houston shared insights about "the marks of a father," which he relates to both natural and spiritual fathers. "A spiritual father," he said, "knows how to discipline his children with mercy, grace, and love." In 1 Samuel 4, Eli did not correct his sons, even though they had been involved in immorality and had not been following God's commands concerning sacrifices and offerings. The result was the downfall of Eli's ministry. On his watch, the ark of the Lord, which represented the presence of God, was stolen from the temple. In that same regard, a spiritual father is able to discern his true sons and daughters, those who are faithful, won't leave when disciplined, and will protect the DNA and reputation of the ministry.

Mike also quoted the apostle Paul when he talked about the importance of a father's travailing prayers for his children:

My dear children, for whom I am again in the pains of childbirth until Christ is formed in you.   (Galatians 4:19 NIV)

"Some things will come to pass," Mike says, "only if a father is pressing in through the pain of travailing, the pain of prayer, and the pain of fasting. Lots of spiritual fathers complain about their children or the staff God has sent to them. As fathers, they know the destinies of their children, but they do not always go to war for those destinies."

Rusty Griffin, pastor of Christian City Fellowship in Sealy, Texas, put it this way: "Many times, there is a treasure inside a youth's heart, but he doesn't recognize it, so he runs after the treasure in someone else's heart. A spiritual father has to help him see the treasure in his own heart."

I remember when Ruben began coming to the ministry and was insecure about his reading ability. I encouraged him to get his GED, which he did, and now he preaches and teaches the Bible at our weekly worship service when I'm away. Likewise, I saw how Kathy had a gift for counseling, so I encouraged her to get training. Now God uses her gift daily as she ministers to people who call in or come to our office for help with material, emotional, and physical needs.

Curt Williams of Youth-Reach Houston shares another real-life illustration of coming alongside the youth in a practical way:

During one of our many projects at Youth-Reach, I was in need of a specific tool to complete a job. I looked over at one of the boys, a resident of only a month or so, who likely had never held a tool in his life, and asked him to get me a crescent wrench from our workshop. He said "OK" and took off to get it for me. A few minutes later, he returned. Without saying a word, he held out to me a set of Channellock pliers. I could see in his eyes that he had probably looked at all the tools on the wall in the workshop and had just guessed that this was what I had asked for. It was also clear that he was really hoping he had guessed right.

He wanted to please me, and he had tried his best. You see, many of our boys arrive in baggy clothes with a gang affiliation and a long arrest record. They appear tough, but plain old hard work reveals that they are weak and soft and lack basic knowledge of how to really be a man.

I left the project behind and took that boy with me to the workshop. Without embarrassing him, I went over all the tools hanging there on the wall. He drank it all in and asked questions whenever he did not grasp the use of each tool. It was so clear that, at that moment, something had been missing in his life, or, more specifically, *someone* had been missing.

His father should have been teaching him this, but it was not to be. That man had abandoned him. However, it was my personal joy to step into the role of daddy for just a few minutes.

I have had the honor of doing this with hundreds of abandoned boys. It is important to teach young men the Word of God. It is also important to teach them how to hold a hammer, how to speak to girls, and how to balance a checkbook. These are simple life lessons, but without a father, who will teach them?

We are experiencing the fallout of a nation that has found it acceptable to procreate at will and then abandon its offspring. This generation of boys is looking for daddies; and if we, the church, can look beyond our programs and buildings, we will find a generation of world changers right outside our doors. But do we really care enough to pay the emotional, spiritual, and financial costs required to reclaim them? The answer to that question is yet to be heard.

MY GREATEST JOY

One of my greatest joys is to hear members of the younger generation tell me how they feel empowered when I come to visit them in their ministries. They feel valued and validated by a spiritual father. God has used me, someone who had no idea how to be a father in the natural, to spiritually father many.

I led Randy to the Lord in 1981, and he proudly calls himself "the first Turning Pointer" after the name of our parent ministry, Turning Point Ministries International, which began as a Bible study in my workout studio. Randy was a professional dancer at the time and had been the Texas disco champion. Now he leads Ad Deum dance company, which has a troupe that tours the world and dances for the glory of God.

Once when I returned from an international trip, I had voice mail message that Randy had left for me on Father's Day. "This is your son, Randall," he said. "I just wanted to thank you for being such a good father and friend. You raised me well."

Michael also calls me every Father's Day. One year, he left a beautiful letter for me at the office, thanking me for being a spiritual father, not even knowing how much I needed that encouragement at the moment.

J. T. is another spiritual son from the early days of the ministry. His father had been shot and killed years earlier, and the anger, pain, and desire for revenge had held him hostage. But after J. T. came to know his heavenly Father and received the Spirit of adoption through the salvation of Christ, he was able to forgive his father and walk in that forgiveness. Today, he is a successful businessman, husband, and father, and he serves on our board of directors. His daughter calls me "Uncle Dougie."

Russ was addicted to drugs as a young man, and his family contacted me when they had nowhere else to turn. I was able to minister to him and help him get into a program. "Thanks to you," he wrote to me once, "my kids never had to see their dad drunk or on drugs. You are an example of what I aspire to be."

Dale was a part of our ministry for many years before moving back to Pittsburgh. In 2004, I had the privilege of reading Scriptures at his wedding. He was fifty-three and marrying for the first time. During the weekend's festivities, I was honored when he publicly shared that he had two spiritual fathers: One was the late John Osteen, and the other was me.

Monica now serves at a nearby church pastored by one of my friends. Although I could not be there when they ordained her for ministry, I wrote a letter that was read during the ceremony, giving her a father's blessing and letting her know how proud of her I am. She told me later the letter had brought tears to her eyes. She wanted her "daddy" to come when she graduated with her master's degree, as well.

Kathy never knew her biological father, and her mother died when she was young. She came to our ministry in 1996 during Prayer Mountain, a citywide gathering of prayer, worship, and fasting, which we hosted the last forty days of that year. Obeying God's prompting, she began volunteering for us and later came on staff. When she was going through a season of personal difficulties and was abandoned by her husband, God allowed me to spiritually father her by insuring that she would be taken care of financially through her employment with the ministry. Now Kathy ministers to the singles at her church and even has her own ministry to widows. She never misses an opportunity to honor me as one of her fathers.

Cindy was a teenager struggling with rejection and thoughts of suicide when the Lord led her to a Catholic church where we presented the gospel through one of our dramas, and she gave her life to Jesus that night. Now her husband is active in our men's ministry and she has three beautiful daughters who come with her when she volunteers in the office.

And the list goes on: Ruben, Cynthia, Tim, Mike, Michael, Lance, Kevin, Jeremy, Jamie, Laura, Andrew, John, Debbie, Marti, Bob, Scott—so many people have acknowledged me as one of their spiritual fathers. What a gift!

In *Hope for a Fatherless Generation*, I quoted Dr. Cole's definition of a father. He said, "A father is the one who guides, guards, and governs in the home. He is the one who brings proper disciplines, strengths, and direction to the family unit."[17]

Let us be fathers who will be remembered with adoration for our discipline, strength, and love.

LEADING BY EXAMPLE

Leading by example is a major component of God's plan for older generations. Something is desperately wrong when one generation is unable to successfully transmit its values to its children and grandchildren. The scriptural norm is found in Psalm 145:4–5 (NIV):

> *One generation commends your works to another; they tell of your mighty acts. They speak of the glorious splendor of your majesty.*

God wants us to be the kind of leaders whom younger generations commend to others. He wants one of our top priorities to be sharing the gospel and power of God with those we father and mother, both naturally and spiritually.

But even many intact families are finding it difficult to convince their children to accept their values. In fact, through the National Study of Youth and Religion, researchers concluded, "Most teenagers believe in a combination of works [based] righteousness, religion as psychological well-being, and a distant non-interfering god."[18]

17. Doug Stringer, *Hope for a Fatherless Generation* (Shippensburg, PA: Destiny Image, 1995, 2009), 25.
18. Gene Edward Veith, "A Nation of Deists," WorldMag.com, June 25, 2005, http://www.worldmag.com/2005/06/a_nation_of_deists.

How could this be? Why do so many Christian parents struggle to raise children who are radically committed to Christ? The answer is sad to admit: Many of us have lived lukewarm, uninspiring Christian lives, which are unappealing to our children. They see our compromise and conclude that they don't want what we have. Really, who can blame them? Hypocritical Christianity isn't very attractive.

The writer of Hebrews tells us that there is a "great cloud of witnesses" in the great "Hall of Faith" that is watching us from the grandstands.

> *And all these, having obtained a good testimony through faith, did not receive the promise, God having provided something better for us, that they should not be made perfect apart from us. Therefore we also, since we are surrounded by so great a cloud of witnesses, let us lay aside every weight, and the sin which so easily ensnares us, and let us run with endurance the race that is set before us.*
>
> (Hebrews 11:39–12:1)

Isn't it amazing that the great heroes of faith will be made perfect *"only together with us"* (NIV)? In the same way, our own destinies are inextricably tied to both those who have preceded us and those who will follow us in the relay race of life. Therefore, no task is more important than successfully passing on our faith to the next generation.

Leonard Ravenhill once told our staff, "Starting with only one hundred twenty people in the upper room, the early Christians had no Bibles, concordances, seminaries, church buildings, or modern media; but they had an endowment of power from on high. With scarcely any human resources, they turned the world upside down. Today, in contrast, we have more than one hundred twenty million believers who claim to be filled with the Holy Spirit; yet we have generally failed to turn the world upside down. We have all the resources, money, and Bible colleges; yet we lack a genuine endowment of spiritual power."

We have a nation full of concordances and Bibles that collect dust, but God is investing His anointing in men and women of character so that they can affect and infect a whole generation, redeeming young people who have been spiritually aborted and abandoned by a self-centered society and an often apathetic church. The spiritual battle for the moral souls of this generation should move us to realign our priorities and carry out the biblical mandate of every believer to be a tangible expression of Christ.

The kingdom of God is built on relationships. Our love as followers of Christ is reflected in the kindness and compassion we show others. Yet, far too often, we are so engulfed in our personal challenges that we neglect the very things that attract God's favor and blessings.

We live in such an impersonal, systems-structured society. As a result, instead of people imitating us as we imitate Christ, they become clones of modern-day institutional Christianity. They are "programmed" by our church structures and activities, which are often much too similar to the world they left behind.

The spiritual battle for the moral souls of this generation should move us to realign our priorities and carry out the biblical mandate of every believer to be a tangible expression of Christ.

The present young generation needs to see that we are who we say we are. They need to see us walk the talk. They need to see that we are the same people at home as we are at church. They need to see that we are different from the world.

If we display the fruits of the character of God—not bitterness and anger—when responding to trouble, then our walk will begin to speak, inspire, and direct. It will bring vision and hope to a generation that hungers for substance.

THE DESIRE FOR CONNECTION

Recently, I gained some insight into how we pass along that vision and hope; namely, through the biblical practice of laying on of hands.

Even though, in the New Testament, hands were laid on people to impart healing and ordain them into the ministry, one of the original roots of the practice was to pass on blessing from one generation to another, as Jacob did with his sons.

Laying on of hands is not something you can do by phone, e-mail, or text. You have to be present. One of the tragedies many young people face is that they don't have parents who are truly there for them in person or by example. They don't have present dads and moms who can impart to them the value or even the techniques of interaction.

They are, however, very skilled with technology! These young people can find their way around the latest electronic devices—computers, iPods, cell phones—with ease. This often comes, though, at the cost of personal intimacy.

Contrast this with my generation, which grew up with board games and athletics as recreational activities. We relied on personal visits, telephone calls, and even written letters to keep in touch, and our communities were built around churches and schools. Whether we had model or absent parents, we still knew our neighbors. Our relationships were personal. This interdependent mentality dates back to when our country was founded, when entire communities were centered around the church and the water well—the two places of "life."

These young people can find their way around the latest electronic devices with ease. This often comes, though, at the cost of personal intimacy.

A staff associate told the story of three young brothers sitting on a couch, each playing with his own Game Boy. They were in the same room, sitting side by side on the sofa, yet there was no interaction, no conversation, no communication. We see it on a larger scale, as well, at internet cafés and coffee shops filled with young people working on their own laptops, not interacting with one another but obviously feeling the need to be connected via a social setting. Then there's the popularity of social media sites like Instagram and Twitter, by which kids can connect with one another via cyberspace. "I've seen Facebook profiles of kids who have five thousand 'friends,'" said my friend Mike. "There are people in every generation who are very relational and people in every generation who are very withdrawn. The danger today is that young people can have relationships without any personal interaction."

In their hearts, Mike says, they are crying out to be part of something, longing to be connected. They just don't always know how to do it. That they frequent coffeehouses and cybercafes confirms an innate desire to be connected to a bigger picture.

THE PERSONAL TOUCH

I prefer the personal touch. I don't like voice mail or voice-prompt menus. But we live in such an impersonal society, even in our churches. We need to get back to the personal touch, because God is a personal God.

An Australian television commercial depicts a young Japanese couple in the delivery room celebrating the arrival of their newborn baby.

"How cute!" say the doctors and nurses to the proud parents. As the camera moves in to show viewers the sweet face of the little one wrapped snuggly in his blanket, the newborn suddenly whips out a Fuji camera and takes a picture of his surprised and astonished parents! The inferred message, of course, is that all Japanese are born with a camera in their hands.

Although I was born in Japan and my mother was Japanese, I don't exactly fit this typical Asian stereotype. I didn't even own a digital camera until I received one for my forty-eighth birthday from a church whose pastor wanted me to get back to my Asian roots.

Instead, you could probably say that I was born with a phone in my ear instead of a camera in my hands. People say that I'm always on the phone, and that's because I love to keep in touch with people. No matter what time of day or night I happen to be awake, I know that there is someone in the world—whether in Malaysia, Africa, Fiji, Australia, or some other part of the US—I can call on the phone, just to let them know that I am thinking about them.

When it comes to technology, we need the younger generation to teach us their knowledge, skill, and finesse. And, in turn, we can impart to them the gifts of personal touch and face-to-face interaction.

Matt and his wife, Katy, coordinate a youth initiative throughout the Northeast. I had been the keynote speaker for their outreach in that same community. Several of the interns had ministered to me during a time of prayer led by Matt and Katy's ten-year-old son, Caleb, who had been a pivotal part of the outreach with his energy, zeal, and enthusiasm. Just a few days after I had left, Caleb had been in a car accident and had gone home to be with Jesus. Josh had also been in the accident but survived.

When it comes to technology, we need the younger generation to teach us their knowledge, skill, and finesse. And, in turn, we can impart to them the gifts of personal touch and face-to-face interaction.

A year later, Matt told me how he demonstrated the love of God to his oldest son, Joshua, who was twelve at the time. One day, during an outreach in Lowell, Massachusetts, the teams of young people were in an intense time of prayer and worship. They had been out all day serving the community with work projects. Josh, still reeling from all that had happened, went off by himself, feeling tired, fearful, and confused. As Matt tells the story:

> Knowing Josh had suffered a loss no twelve-year-old can easily endure, I walked up behind him and put my hand on his shoulder. He was slouched in his seat, and his face was covered so no one would see him crying. I leaned over to gently speak in his ear and asked, "What's wrong?"

"I don't know."

I knew that meant I should ask again. "What's the matter?"

He told me that he felt scared, like God was far away from him. The Holy Spirit quickened me to ask, "Do you know how close God is?"

"No."

I quickly replied, "He is this close." Then I knelt down and hugged him as long and as hard as I could. Josh didn't need my theology or thoughts at that point. He needed a tangible understanding of how much God loves him and how close He really is.

Later that evening, he thanked me and asked, "What do kids do when they feel far from God and don't have a dad to hold them?" Even in his youth, Josh recognized the need for human touch, for the tangible touch of a father.

One Christmas, a team of five families from Warren, Pennsylvania, came to Houston, giving up their own holiday to serve others in our Holiday of Hope ministry and other Christmas outreaches. As one of the dads on the team was helping a five-year-old girl and her mom pick out Christmas toys in our fellowship hall, the little girl looked up to him and asked, "Could you give me a hug for my daddy? I don't have a daddy." He hugged her and tried to hold back his tears.

God depends on us to be fathers in the flesh to those who don't have dads to hold them. Let us not be afraid to impart this intimacy and to "be there" in person and by example. It was no mistake God chose to pass on blessings through the laying on of hands!

6

MOMMIES, DADDIES, AND DAUGHTERS

Whlen we think of the effects of fatherlessness, we often think in terms of the father-son relationship and the impact it has on men. But we would be remiss to neglect the detrimental effect the lack of fathers has on women in our society.

During a tour of a juvenile justice center, one of our staff members was told that dealing with juvenile girls is among their biggest and fastest growing problems. They're constantly getting in trouble. They're angry, violent, uncontrollable, and mentally unstable. "You can't put them into a residential facility," he was told. "They'll run away. They're just unruly." There is also a growing number of juvenile girls involved in gangs.

County officials have identified two primary issues at the heart of all these problems. The first problem is diet. When a person doesn't care about herself, and believes no one else does, she will not care what she eats. Such people often turn to food for comfort. The second problem is men. Most of the girls have issues with their fathers. They're looking for an identity, so they get involved in bad relationships or gangs. They give their bodies to boys who use them and break their hearts. Sadly, the cycle continues until they feel that they have nothing to live for.

Socialization and finding identity are necessary processes, but they are definitely harder when the family unit is fragmented, giving no parameters to help define the God-given roles of parent, daughter, and sister. Without a place to find identity, young people create their own worlds and families. Sometimes this occurs by joining gangs. We see it with street kids, too, who create their own family dynamics and even find identity in their "street names."

"Covering" is a church term for the sense of protection we feel, both spiritually and physically. Spiritually, the Bible tells us that the moment we receive Christ, a canopy of protection is stretched out over our lives. We see this truth pictured in the description of the Passover. While the children of Israel were preparing to flee Egypt, a spirit of death was being released against the firstborn of the land. The only protection for Israel was the shed blood of a spotless lamb on the doorposts of their dwellings. If the blood was in place, they were spared. (See Exodus 12:21–27.) Today, Christ is our Passover Lamb. (See 1 Corinthians 5:7.) His blood keeps us safe and secure. This is the glorious work of the cross in our lives and the inheritance of every believer.

When there is a breach of covering in our physical, earthly lives, we feel exposed, vulnerable, and even unwanted. When a woman feels uncovered by her husband, there is disarray in the home. When a girl feels uncovered by her parents, especially by her father, she looks elsewhere to find the strength God designed to come from him. She looks for identity in places outside the realm of God's intended plan. And when a girl has not experienced the love of a father, she will look to other men for that love.

One of my daughters in the faith, Laura, ministers to young women all over the world, and she also has an ongoing group that meets in her home. Before her father went to be with Jesus, he had asked me to help watch over Laura and her mother, and now she considers me a spiritual father.

When a girl has not experienced the love of a father, she will look to other men for that love.

Laura said, "A few years ago, the Lord opened my eyes to the desperate need of this generation's young women, and how they need to be spiritually mothered and fathered."

"I found myself surrounded by the most beautiful, precious young women. They all loved the Lord passionately and wanted nothing more than to please Him. As I developed sweet friendships with these precious souls, I began to hear their stories. To my sad surprise, almost all of them were stories of woundedness and brokenness."

Laura asked me to speak to the young ladies she mentors, believing that I could minister God's healing heart to heal them from their "daddy issues." I spoke to them with the heart of a father, repented to them on behalf of any men who had hurt them, and released them into their destinies by praying over them and giving them a father's blessing.

One of the girls in the group, Adriana, has not seen her biological father since she was five years old, and she shared her story with us:

I remember all the adventurous things I did with my father as if it was yesterday. He was full of energy when I was five years old, and he always knew how to plan our day. My day started with my dad dressing me, brushing my hair, and walking me to school. He didn't have to do these things, but he did them because he wanted to. He considered me his pride and joy because I was his only daughter. Our day would end after school when he would pick me up and we would walk back through a small bayou where I would catch guppies in a sandwich bag. There are so many memories I have of my dad! I never want to lose them because they are all I have.

Life does not always end up the way you would like it, especially when your parents divorce. I never really understood how much of an impact it had on my life until now. For so long, I never cared to know the true story about why my dad had left, because I was angry at him; and my mom never knew how to explain, so she left it all unknown. As the years went by and I grew older, I desired a relationship with him once again. But how do you pick up where you left off when someone has been gone since you were five?

I am twenty-four years old now, and as I replay situations in my life that brought about terrible consequences, I know they were a result of not having my father. I had no male role model, so I ran to men to satisfy that void in my life. I found myself in relationships with the wrong men, but I was so afraid to be abandoned again that I stayed with them to feel safe and protected. I never knew the difference between a good man and a bad man; I knew only that I felt loved and that I belonged to someone. I have been in the worst relationships with physical, emotional, and mental abuse, but I stayed in them because I thought I needed a man to complete me.

If my dad had been around, I don't think I would have gone through these things, because a father offers his strength and wisdom to help his daughter(s) choose the right man.

Recently, my dreams of seeing my dad again nearly came true. I was invited to California with a friend, so I accepted in hopes of seeing my dad. I contacted him, and we talked about plans of driving to Fresno to meet him halfway. You can imagine my excitement! I began preparing a photo album with pictures of me growing up and pictures of me now, just to help us catch up. I was expecting to meet him on Friday morning after we flew into San Diego, but the week before I left, I called his house phone but could not get an answer. I left three messages for him.

By Thursday, I realized it was not going to happen, and I was right. I cried, and I began to question why he would do this to me and not even call me. I still do not know the real story, but I know that the day will come for me to see him again. It seems to me that nineteen years is long enough to wait, but God knows best, and I trust His timing to be perfect.

In the meantime, I look back in my life, and I see how God has blessed me with my stepfather, who has done so much for my family. I also see how He placed other men of God in my path to stand in the gap as spiritual fathers—men like Pastor Doug Stringer. His words and prayers have blessed me so much, especially when he helped me realize that my Father in heaven has been here for me all these years!

Even though my biological father was not present to see all the things I have feared and overcome, my heavenly Father was there holding my hand, giving me all the strength I needed.

I see many similarities between Adriana's testimony and my own. My parents, too, divorced when I was a child. As a young man, I felt the desperate void of his absence. I left my mother and stepfather's house and lived an aimless life for a period, sleeping on freight trains and donating plasma so I could have money to eat.

Eventually, I determined to find my father and discovered that he lived in Houston. I moved there and found him, but it did not fill the void. Like Adriana, I found that the search for my father led me to my heavenly Father.

Even with the similarities in our testimonies, we must still acknowledge God's design in creating men and women to be different. Our needs are different, our giftings are different, and our wounds are different. And as the body of Christ, we must respond to women accordingly.

REPENTANCE AND RELEASE

Many fathers, husbands, and even spiritual authorities do not treat women with respect. This produces a ripple effect, sending waves of oppression, suppression, and all kinds of abuse across society. Atrocities occur across the globe as women are raped, forced to have abortions, inflicted with mandated traditional rites of passage, and abandoned by irresponsible men. Emptiness, shame, and unworthiness have hindered many women. They are hurting, and we need to bring healing. They must be released to wholeness in Christ, but this requires repentance on the part of men. We must repent for the sins against women and begin to speak against the injustice women face around the world.

At the 2001 Global Celebration of Women in Houston, I was able to stand in the gap of repentance toward all attending women.

"On behalf of all the men who have ever hurt you," I said, "verbally or physically abused you, or who even kept you oppressed in the name of religion, please forgive us. Perhaps you've been held back from fulfilling your destiny, or you've been made to feel like a second-class citizen. But ladies, the Lord Himself looks at you and says, 'I have a destiny to accomplish through those who surrender to Me.'"

Many tearful women came to me at the conclusion of the meeting saying things like, "I finally got set free tonight" and "I understand that I have a destiny." I reported what happened at this meeting to a ministry friend in Atlanta. She began to cry over the phone and said, "What you shared at that citywide prayer meeting set me free."

I delivered a similar message at the 2005 Inspire Women's Rally in Houston, where I was privileged to be the first male keynote speaker. Over two thousand women from a wide variety of denominations and ethnic backgrounds came together. Afterward, many of them said that they felt like a spiritual father had blessed them and released them into their future.

The more we operate in this prophetic act of repentance, the more we will release the body of Christ into its destiny. The world is desperately searching for answers, and it's going to take both men and women to fulfill God's plan.

I believe that America will experience revival either through a birthing or a shaking. I relate the process we're in to the birth process, in which a woman needs strength to deliver a healthy child. Earlier, we quoted King Hezekiah, who said, "This is a day of trouble and distress because the children are ready to be born but there's no strength to deliver them." (See Isaiah 37:3.)

For a healthy baby to be born, there must be a healthy womb; and for a healthy womb, there must be a healthy woman; and for a healthy woman, there must be a relationship with her heavenly Father. Furthermore, there must be a relationship with a healthy man who is not intimidated by her gifts and who can and will give her strength to deliver.

Men are meant to be strength-givers to women. Yet for different reasons, men have allowed insecurities and fears to hinder them, which has created problems that have trickled down through society. Women have been vulnerable, forsaken, and, in some ways, devalued.

When men become secure in their identities in Christ however, they aren't threatened by the gifts of women. They are able to bless them and release them to become all that God destined for them to be.

Proverbs 31:3 says, *"Do not give your strength to women."* This means that men should not abdicate the strength God has given them by stepping out of their roles and leaving women to take on more responsibilities than God intended for them. It means to not be a wimp made in America—or in my case, Japan.

When men become secure in their identities in Christ, they aren't threatened by the gifts of women. They are able to bless them and release them to become all that God destined for them to be.

However, we cannot go to the other extreme by being harsh and abusive. Jesus is saying, "Don't give away your strength—be a strength." Men were designed to guide, protect, encourage, and strengthen women. Women were created to be life-givers and nurturers. So, men, if we want to have healthy births and life-giving, nurturing care for an entire generation, we need to release women to fulfill their destinies, and we also need godly men who are secure in Christ to come alongside them as strength-givers, so that, together, we will be a powerful, positive force for God's kingdom. We need the Spirit of Christ to empower us! It's going to take all of us to go from death to life, from tragedy to triumph.

JESUS SHOWED THE WAY

Jesus knew how to strengthen both men and women and release them into their ministries. When He spoke to the Samaritan woman at the well, He went against society's norms in two ways: He talked to both a Samaritan and a woman. Even the disciples questioned what He was doing. But no one could deny that this woman received not only an answer to her questions but also a new life. She was affirmed, empowered, and released to proclaim the good news: She declared, *"Come, see a Man"* (John 4:29)!

Like the Samaritan woman, many women today need affirmation. Emotional and spiritual barrenness have stripped them of their very feminine attributes, thus resulting in a barren generation, as well.

Women are marrying later in life and are establishing careers first and family second. They are approaching their thirties and forties without bearing children. Furthermore, many men fear commitment, and their reaction to the women's movement was to pull away from relationships.

Many women today need affirmation. Emotional and spiritual barrenness have stripped them of their very feminine attributes, thus resulting in a barren generation, as well.

Today we are as desperate for God to fill our empty wombs as Hannah was for Him to fill hers. (See 1 Samuel 1:11.) A barren woman who greatly desired a son, Hannah regularly poured out her heart to God at the altar, reminding Him of her affliction. Once, when she was crying out in the house of the Lord, Eli the prophet brought her encouragement and gave her hope. When God answered the travail of her heart, Hannah gave birth to a new generation of prophets who would prepare the way for the coming of the Lord through her son, Samuel.

Today, there's a generation of prophets and prophetesses both in the natural and in the spirit realm yet to be born. They're ready to come forth; but we, the church, need strength to deliver them.

Hannah's husband, Elkanah, represents the type of covering we men are to provide. He comforted Hannah, stood by her, and blessed her even in her despair and labor. Men of God must support, nurture, and encourage women. We must undergird the women of our generation. When we do this, the Valley of Baca, or the valley of weeping, will become a spring. (See Psalm 84:6.) Streams of living water will gush forth, providing a lasting drink to quench every thirst.

The well where Jesus met the Samaritan woman was not just any watering place. It was Jacob's well, and from it sprang living waters that quenched the thirsts of generations. As the women of our day receive the same revelation and freedom as the Samaritan woman, their nights of weeping will cease, and together the body of Christ will declare, "*Come, see a Man*"!

BIRTHING A GENERATION

Our world needs a birth of resurrection life that will lead to revival and a harvest of thousands upon thousands of souls. Something is getting ready to happen, and we need to PUSH—Pray Until Something Happens—for the release of a generation living on the edge for Christ. We need men, women, and children together to become all God wants them to be. God needs all of us—regardless of race, status, age, or gender—to orchestrate His will upon the earth. Both men and women are needed for prayer and spiritual warfare. Scripture says,

> *There is neither Jew nor Greek, there is neither slave nor free, there is neither male nor female; for you are all one in Christ Jesus.*
> (Galatians 3:28)

We need the passion and zeal of the young; the life-giving, nurturing nature of women; and the strong, protective, and empowering attributes of men. To give birth to revival, the whole army of God needs to combine their gifts and strengths.

It's time for us to rise up with the radical determination and conviction of Joan of Arc, an inexperienced warrior whose enthusiasm inspired the entire French army, which no king had been able to do. During battle, she approached the general of the army and stated emphatically, "I'm going to lead the men over the wall."

The general replied, "There isn't one man who is going to follow you."

With her eyes fixed like flint, seventeen-year-old Joan replied, "I wouldn't know. I don't plan on looking back to check." She took off over the wall, and every one of the men followed. Her courageous example delivered her country.

Birthing revival will require the same kind of heroism and radical commitment in the hearts of those who bear the gospel of good news today.

Just as Jesus approached the Samaritan woman at the well, He's approaching you and me. The challenges, barriers, and limitations placed on us are now in the past. It's time to allow the Lord to heal us. He's not ashamed to call us His children. He's not embarrassed of who we are. He created us in His image. We must release our past and run with the vision God has placed on our heart. He has a purpose for our lives!

If we allow Him to change our hearts, we will experience a new birth. And after the baby is born, we'll forget the pain, the sorrow, and the obstacles; we'll rejoice in what the Lord has done. (See John 16:20–22.)

Identifying and utilizing the strengths of each generation and each gender, we'll become what I term "Gen-Edge" people—a generation living on the edge for Christ. Functioning in God's design and order, we all will benefit as we benefit His kingdom.

IT'S TIME TO HAVE A BABY!

God is calling His people to become fathers and mothers to the fatherless. He is calling men to rise up and to be men, to accept their God-given positions in the family and in the church by providing strength, to be husbands to the widows. He wants men of strength, maturity, and integrity to spiritually father sons and daughters. He is calling us forth!

God is giving strength to birth the coming revival. He is birthing a fresh generation with a fresh anointing out of the spiritual womb of His church. They will be a prophetic generation that will not be like the former generations. They will not be like their fathers.

> *That the generation to come might know them, the children who would be born, that they may arise and declare them to their children, that they may set their hope in God, and not forget the works of God, but keep His commandments; and may not be like their fathers, a stubborn and rebellious generation, a generation that did not set its heart aright, and whose spirit was not faithful to God.*
> (Psalm 78:6–8)

Instead of being stubborn and rebellious, they will be a generation that puts their hope in God, not succumbing to compromise, but living on the edge for Jesus.

God is ready to bring forth a massive move through the lives of His people. It won't be contained in any one church building, denomination, or even nation. He is doing something exponential. He has put that plan into our spiritual wombs, and He is giving us the strength to bring it forth! Unfulfilled visions, dreams, and passions, which have been locked away for a long time, will now be birthed. Not only are we in labor to bring forth a prophetic generation but the fullness of God's church. It's time for me, and it's time for you. Get ready to birth a lasting revival that will change our world.

As a man of God, I come to all other men with a word of encouragement—the same one that the prophet Eli proclaimed to Hannah—"*Go in peace, and the God of Israel grant your petition which you have asked of Him*" (1 Samuel 1:17).

Fulfill your destiny and take part in the beautiful birth of a prophetic generation. We're in labor; it's time to have a baby!

7

A CHURCH GOD CAN USE

I met Peter and Wes, members of the band Newsboys, when I was asked to speak at a celebration in Houston. We sat together at a pre-event pastors' luncheon and soon discovered a mutual passion to invest in the younger generation.

They told me that over the past ten years, their band has ministered to more than 10 million young people at their concerts. But God has given them a burden to go beyond just pointing youth to Christ; now they desire to help them also build a strong foundation. To do that, the Newsboys partnered with Every Nation Ministries to publish *The Purple Book: Biblical Foundations for Building Strong Disciples*. The book includes a letter from Peter Furler, who wrote,

> Although I grew up in the church, a lot of these foundational principles were not grounded in my life. Memorize and meditate on the Scriptures daily, and teach others to do the same. Together, we will make this generation a people full of the knowledge of God's Word—a people with a strong foundation worth handing down to the next generation.[19]

---

19. Peter Furler quoted in Rice Brooks and Steven Murrell, *The Purple Book: Biblical Foundations for Building Strong Disciples* (Grand Rapids, MI: Zondervan, 2009).

God wants to heal this generation and set them free, but we must first learn what the Newsboys have learned. We must not stop sharing the gospel; we must also go the extra mile to help them grow strong in the faith and reach out to others with the love of God.

THE EXTRA MILE

On any given day, I'll get voice mails at the office from street kids we helped in the early days of the ministry.

"This is your son Jeremy calling. I'm hanging in there. Keep praying for me. I love you, man."

"This is Jamie. My daughter Angel just graduated from kindergarten. Tell everybody I said hello."

"This is Lance. Let Doug know I'm doing OK. I'm going to church and serving in a soup kitchen."

"This is Kevin. Could you send me a Bible?"

When we launched our ministry, we were a radical group of young people, untrained and uneducated, but with a passion to win the lost. We took people into our homes. We went the extra mile. At one time, I had seventeen people staying in my apartment, many of them just like those camels in chapter 2—dirty, thirsty, and smelly. But God gave us hearts to serve them!

The church that will experience true revival is the one who presents herself as the servant bride, the one who is willing to serve the Lord and willing to serve those dirty, smelly, thirsty camels coming out of the wilderness of life.

At the annual banquet for Montrose Street Reach, a young man shared his testimony. Raised in a fatherless home and sexually abused at a young age, he had been living on the streets of Houston as a transvestite prostitute who called himself Olivia. Looking beyond his confused exterior, the ministry's leaders saw him through the eyes of God and pursued him relentlessly. It literally took years, but God's love and persistence finally broke through, and he gave his life to Christ. Today, he lives with a family from a local church and works on the church staff, where he is nurtured and educated in the ways of God. Where would this young man be if Montrose Street Reach and the churches serving with them had not been willing to persevere?

The church that will experience true revival is the one who presents herself as the servant bride, the one who is willing to serve the Lord and willing to serve those dirty, smelly, thirsty camels coming out of the wilderness of life.

Buddy and Carolyn had seen God move in radical ways in the lives of young people during the 1970s and 1980s. With retirement approaching, they served a large church in Humble, Texas, where Buddy served as pastor. They were well taken care of financially, but their hearts were burdened with a passion for the young people of the community. They could no longer be content with business as usual.

Teaming with their daughter and son-in-law, Shari and Mike, they purchased a city block in old downtown Humble where they built a skate park, turned an old gas station into a cybercafe called Fuel, and started Somebody Cares Humble. Secular bands come from all over the area to play at Fuel, even though they have to sign a contract to not drink, swear, or sing inappropriate or ungodly lyrics.

Local teens work and serve in the café and the skate park. They earn college scholarships if they keep their grades up and stay clean from alcohol and drugs. The church has become a youth church called Pipeline, pastored by Mike and Shari. Hundreds of kids have been spiritually fathered in the ministry through what we have termed "pre-conversion discipleship." Many of them would be heading directly down a path of destruction if not for the sacrifice and commitment of this family.

There are so many others out there doing the same—going the extra mile. Tony got out of Bible college and began doing street ministry in the Deep Ellum area of Dallas. With the purchase of a popular coffeehouse called Insomnia, Tony has helped hundreds of young people from the goth and other subcultures receive ministry on a regular basis, once again through "pre-conversion discipleship." Though it no longer owns the coffeehouse, the ministry is now called "Life in Deep Ellum" and has expanded its outreach to the entire community.

J. J. is a spiritual son in the Lord living and working in College Station, just north of Houston. Save Our Streets (SOS) Ministries reaches out to young people and college students in the area with weekly Bible studies and transitional living for kids who have nowhere else to go. Saved by the Lord from a life of crime and gangs, J. J.'s heart is that no young life slips through the cracks. "I believe that, in a man's life and ministry, he must be pointed out by great men of faith," J. J. wrote to me once. "Even Jesus was pointed out by His Father. You, Doug, came and pointed me out." Now, he is doing the same thing for his own spiritual children.

SOS now partners with Stuart, a medical doctor who heads up Medical Missions International, part of Somebody Cares Brazos Valley. Stuart's ministry was birthed when God spoke to him at one of my Bible studies to use his medical gifts to help the people of Africa.

Years ago, in Stafford, Texas, God gave EZ and Lena a vision for young people, so they started Generation Jesus. Today, the ministry is equipping a radical group of young people to impact their community through their church, The Epicenter.

Gideon and Sara minister to Asian Indians and other young people at Houston Baptist University. Jeremy heads up Generation Xcel and coordinated the youth outreach for Billy Graham's New York City Crusade. Mike launched Firehouse Cyber Café with a vision to keep it open twenty-four hours a day so that young people would always have a place to go.

And let's not forget those rescuing lives through adoption of babies and children. In 2001, there were eight hundred adoptable children in the Harris County, Texas, foster care system. Somebody Cares Houston spearheaded Hope in Houston, an adoption awareness campaign. YWAM Houston, which oversaw the campaign for us, has carried on the vision by opening an adoption agency in our offices.

Buddy and Carolyn's daughter and son-in-law were first to adopt through YWAM; their baby was born to a youth from Houston's Montrose area. Buddy and Carolyn had ministered to street kids in Montrose in the 1970s, and now their first grandchild is a fruit of seeds they planted years ago!

Others, too, have stepped up to the plate. Henry and Delia served in our ministry for many years and adopted a foster child. The Byerleys actually inspired our awareness campaign. When Mr. Bylerley first came to me, he and his wife had seventeen children—ten of their own and seven adopted. "If you don't do something to get the word out about the foster children who need to be adopted," he said to me, "my wife is going to adopt all eight hundred of them!"

Going the extra mile does not come without a price. The Byerleys are not wealthy people, and their actions are motivated solely by good hearts. These kids come from troubled backgrounds. Many times, the Byerleys' hearts are broken by the very young people they've sacrificed to help. Yet they have persevered and laid a foundation in these children's lives, so that, when the storms of life come, they can stand on the rock of Jesus Christ.

We've seen our street kids and others die tragically from HIV/AIDS, drive-by shootings, and gang-related violence. Brandy, for example, was a prostitute who died of HIV/AIDS. We arranged and conducted a funeral for her and paid for the burial because she had no family to claim her. Hollywood was a street kid who used to say, "I own these streets." The day before he died in a shooting, he said to a friend, "I need to get my life right with God."

We've grieved over the premature loss of these lives, yet we know that they at least had a chance to call on the name of the Lord. The greatest tragedy is not that these lives have been lost but that so many others are lost without hearing the good news of the gospel. Many young people go through life not knowing where to turn in the tough times.

Today's generation is hungry for love, but are we willing to work with the unlovely? Are we willing to feed them? Will we go the extra mile with them? Will we adopt them, either in the spiritual or in the natural? All too often, the church does not take seriously its responsibility to parent this generation. We give them a lot of platitudes but no spiritual substance. They need to know that, when times get tough, they can call "911 heaven" and connect directly to their Father.

All too often, the church does not take seriously its responsibility to parent this generation. We give them a lot of platitudes but no spiritual substance.

God is challenging us to get out of our comfort zones and to reach out to the camels in the wilderness. More than this, we must be willing to go the distance with them. God loves them, and with the same love in which He reached out to us, we must reach out to them.

RIVERS OF REVIVAL

There is an orphaned and fatherless generation living within a nation that has divorced its godly foundations. But that very generation will see God's grace poured out in one of the greatest revivals we have ever seen. Why? Because God Himself will adopt this generation.

There is an orphaned and fatherless generation living within a nation that has divorced its godly foundations.

Nothing can hinder the plans of God. This generation is the group in which the exponential anointings of the Old Testament will converge, thus preparing a people to go forth into their destinies as they prepare the way for the coming of the Lord. God intends to release a massive outpouring of His Spirit that will transcend every denominational and ethnic background.

We, the church, must come alongside them and stand with them.

God does not judge the world today as He did in Noah's day but instead desires His spotless bride to be an ark of refuge for a world seeking safety. In so doing, an army of laborers will be released, or birthed, from the church into the world.

Your people shall be volunteers in the day of Your power; in the beauties of holiness, from the womb of the morning, You have the dew of Your youth. (Psalm 110:3)

God will use this generation to transform every element of culture and subculture, from media to arts to education to business. They will sign up to volunteer in God's army, to serve the Lord and the nations in love and compassion.

The Bible says that there will be such a move of God that the church walls will not be able to contain it. (See Zechariah 2:4.) It will be like trying to contain a fire burning wider and wider, gathering more and more people in its wake.

God's wall of fire will burn away the chaff and purify a people who are willing to consecrate themselves to Him. The church that God is looking for is one that is already serving a hurting generation. That is the kind of church on which He will pour out His Spirit.

ACCEPTING WHO GOD SENDS

Peter Ferrara, associate professor of law at George Mason University School of Law in Northern Virginia, wrote,

An American is English, or French, or Italian, Irish, German, Spanish, Polish, Russian or Greek. An American may also be Mexican, African, Indian, Chinese, Japanese, Australian, Iranian, Asian, or Arab, or Pakistani, or Afghan.[20]

I'm proud of my Japanese heritage, but I'm not Japanese first; I'm American. But even above that, I'm Christian. The blood of Jesus is pumping through me now, and I share an identity with the body of

20. Peter Ferrara, "What Is an American?" *The National Review*, September 2001.

Christ. We may differ in color on the outside, but we all have the same Spirit on the inside. Our common identity is in Jesus!

The Bible says that we are to run the race to obtain all He has for us (see 1 Corinthians 9:24–25), and I'm of the "obtaining race"! I stand with my brothers and sisters, sharing a common identity in Christ, and look toward the upward call of God. (See Philippians 3:14.)

Hatred and racism run more rampant than ever in the world, and division is commonplace. But the true last-day revival in the house of the Lord will include people from all nations, and it will happen when we put aside differences, lay down our weapons, and gather at the house of the Lord, declaring, "We are brothers and sisters, we love God, and we love one another."

Hatred and racism run more rampant than ever in the world, and division is commonplace. But the true last-day revival in the house of the Lord will include people from all nations, and it will happen when we put aside differences, lay down our weapons, and gather at the house of the Lord.

This generation may come with pierced eyebrows, noses, and foreheads. They may come from every nation, every race. They may be outcast, lame, and sick. They may have stinky breath and matted hair. It doesn't matter. They're coming in—they're thirsty and hungry—and we must serve them. As we do, God will change their nature and transform their lives, and they will become the prophetic generation He intended them to be. But it's up to us to serve them and invite them to gather at the mountain of the Lord.

The principles in God's Word can be applied to any generation—they transcend generational barriers. But we must be willing to accept each generation even with their differences. For example, their styles of worship, dress, music, and behavior may not be what we are accustomed to, but we must see them through God's eyes and love them unconditionally. We must adopt them and welcome them into our family with open arms.

Adrienne S. Gaines writes,

> "Generation Y" is surprising some observers as they demonstrate a unique willingness to build friendship and community with people of all racial backgrounds. Indeed, this group of young men and women, born after 1982, are more crosscultural from birth—many are from mixed racial heritage and 36 percent are 'non-white,' according to *Millennials Rising: The Next Great Generation* by Neil Howe and William Strauss. Though they've been described by the media as materialistic and spoiled, as Christians, they are quickly answering the call to impact our cities—and the world—for Christ. Many of their predecessors, the Generation Xers, have emerged as ministry leaders, acting as Moses to this group of courageous Joshuas.
>
> But will they take us into the Promised Land on the issue of biblical unity? Hope springs eternal.[21]

God is going to pour out His Spirit upon all flesh, and we will see a radical "John the Baptist" generation rise up, which will do mighty exploits for God. Are we willing to serve them? Are we willing to accept them for who they are, as is, without judgment and with no strings attached? Are we willing to invite them in regardless of their background? God sees our potential, and He is calling us to love as Christ loved. (See John 13:34; Ephesians 5:2.)

God calls His church to unity. The Father summons us to accept whatever "camels" He sends our way, regardless of their past, appearances, and ethnicity. The church needs to accept whomever He sends.

Sometimes, it's a risky, demanding sacrifice. We must face our own prejudices and fears. If we're willing to allow God to help us deal with them, we can become the kind of church on which He can pour out His Spirit like never before.

---

21. Adrienne S. Gaines, "The Joshua Generation," *Catalyst* magazine, Spring/Summer 2001, 1.

LEARNING FROM OUR PASTS

God wants us to learn from our pasts. He wants to use the wounds of past generations to help shield the future generations. But before we can use our anointings, purposes, and identities to bring healing, we must first know where we have gone wrong. We must uproot the old and replace it with the new; we must uproot the bad and plant and nurture the right.

The truth is, we have the crisis of fatherlessness in America, and we all have to take responsibility for our own choices. We can try to hide behind our dysfunctional, codependent, and victimized generation. We can blame our upbringing, environment, and societal pressures.

Eventually, however, we have to take responsibility and quit playing the blame game. Once we recognize that we need help, we can make a choice to live for the future.

The Bible says,

In those days they shall say no more: "The fathers have eaten sour grapes, and the children's teeth are set on edge." But every one shall die for his own iniquity; every man who eats the sour grapes, his teeth shall be set on edge. (Jeremiah 31:29–30)

This is basically acknowledging that the sins of fathers truly do affect their children, but that's no excuse for children to disobey. Everyone must answer for his own sin and stop blaming his father for his personal evils and flaws. We can't change our pasts, but we can determine our future by the choices we make every day. We need to take responsibility.

My friend Roger served in Vietnam and, within mere minutes of arriving, was blasted by a hand grenade, shot twice, bayoneted, then left to die. He was rushed to a MASH unit, where the medical team examined him and said there was little chance he'd live. If he did live, it would be without some of his limbs. Gangrene was setting in, and amputation would be required. On top of that, Roger had seventy-two shrapnel wounds, and his face was swollen with infection.

In spite of it all, Roger began to recover. Every day, each one of his seventy-two wounds was opened up and scrubbed to make sure the infection was not progressing. If the wounds were left to heal on their own, they would become infected. The pain, he said, was unbearable. Though he could not speak, he silently cried out to God: *God, if there is a God, if You let me live, I'll serve You the rest of my life.*

God's grace poured out on Roger as he made that simple cry. Slowly, the wounds healed, until, one day, the infection was completely gone. Soon the pain was gone, as well, and all that remained were the scars. Roger not only survived but was restored completely. He said that, without God's grace, he wouldn't have made it.

Likewise, we, too, may have memories and scars, but we don't have to hang on to the pain. We can cry out to God, and He will heal us in His infinite grace. The pain we cling to can hold us back from God's greater purposes.

We can cry out to God, and He will heal us in His infinite grace. The pain we cling to can hold us back from God's greater purposes.

Jesus was able to look beyond the suffering of the cross and find the joy set before Him. (See Hebrews 12:2.) Likewise, we must be able to see beyond our circumstances and look to the future God has for us. The only way to receive healing is to let go of the past.

HOPE AND CONSEQUENCES

I have met many people who have suffered because of both their own choices and their parents' choices. I recall one young man who served in our ministry for several years. When John was a teenager, he became heavily involved in drugs. He later accepted Jesus Christ as His Savior but soon returned to a life of drug addiction. During that season, he contracted HIV/AIDS.

When we met him just a few years later, John had been given six months to live. He returned to a relationship with Jesus and, by God's grace, lived an additional three years. During that time, he participated in fourteen mission trips and spoke to many at-risk youth and young adults about the choices they were making. He was a faithful interces-sor for the ministry and for me personally. Though this man's life was cut short due to the consequences of his actions, he had found hope, meaning, and purpose. He left a legacy to the glory of God!

The generation outside the walls of the church looks messed up. The world has labeled them dysfunctional. They are regarded as perma-nently and terminally codependent and hopeless. They are not taught how to claim victory as they are bombarded with mantras like, "Once an alcoholic, always an alcoholic," "Once a drug addict, always an addict," and so forth.

But my Bible says,

If anyone is in Christ, he is a new creation; old things have passed away; behold, all things have become new.   (2 Corinthians 5:17)

I am a new creature in Him! I may still struggle with temptation, but I am now aware of my struggles and know that God will give me the strength to overcome. (See 1 Corinthians 10:13.)

Genuine freedom comes from being secure in God. The Bible says,

Stand fast therefore in the liberty by which Christ has made us free, and do not be entangled again with a yoke of bondage.

(Galatians 5:1)

I am free from bondage, and I am alive in Christ! And in that place of freedom, the pain from my past is gone. The scars still remain, but the pain does not. God healed me, so I am able to operate in His full-ness. I can't use my past as a cop-out, but I can acknowledge where I've come from. God has converted the pain of my past into compassion, and with that compassion, I am equipped to love the unlovable.

God is looking for those who will make themselves available, who will say, "Here am I; send me." (See Isaiah 6:8.) He searches for those who take responsibility for their mistakes, who have learned from their pasts, who accept whom He sends, who go the extra mile. That is the kind of church God can use to father a generation of orphans, emerging from the wilderness.

8

HONOR AND BLESSING

Growing up, I longed for the acceptance, approval, and affirmation of a father. I can remember being at baseball games and wanting so badly for my stepdad to tell me he was proud of me.

Instead, as he always tried to cover up his pains in life with alcohol, he would often come to my games drinking. Rather than affirming me, he would say things that embarrassed me. As an adult, I was able to lead him to Christ and our relationship was healed as I saw his life through the eyes of God. But as a boy, the absence of affirmation was painful to endure. Even now as a grown man trying to be a spiritual father to others, at times I still find myself longing to be affirmed and acknowledged by father figures.

Likewise, this emerging generation is looking for someone with whom they can share their hearts and all the joys and challenges of serving in the kingdom of God. They need guidance, counsel, and direction. They need someone they can go to and say, "Daddy, how did I do?" Like all of us, they need to hear someone say, "That's my girl!" or "That's my boy!"

Even Jesus received verbal affirmation from His Father. When He was baptized in the Jordan River by John the Baptist, a voice came from heaven, saying, *"This is My beloved Son, in whom I am well pleased*" (Matthew 3:17). That was God the Creator, the Father of heaven and earth, giving complete approval and affirmation of His Son before the people.

Likewise, He is saying to those of us in Christ, "That's my boy!" and "That's my girl!" Oh, to hear those words from our Father! God knows our needs, and He knows when we are lacking these things from our earthly fathers. He longs for us to come to Him at those times, asking, "Did I do good?" "Are you proud of me?" And He loves saying to us, "Well done!"

But how can we know that we are pleasing to God? How can we be sure that we are walking in ways that are making Him proud? God's love for us is unconditional; it is not something we earn. We are His sons and daughters if we have been sealed by the Spirit of adoption. But there are principles we can apply to our lives and attractive attributes we can practice. Though there are many listed throughout Scripture, I often teach on holiness, humility, honesty, and honor.

Holiness is not following some external, religious formula or legalistic piety but submission and surrender of our hearts to the Creator of the universe, who so loved us that He gave His only Son for us. (See John 3:16.) Holiness is our worshipful response, an act of love. It is not an external show or façade but an attitude of the heart. God wants us to walk in humility yet to be confident in who we are in Him. Humility precedes exaltation.

Therefore humble yourselves under the mighty hand of God, that He may exalt you in due time. (1 Peter 5:6)

God wants us to be people of honesty so that we can discern between the spirit of truth and the spirit of error. (See 1 John 4:4–6.) Scripture makes it clear that dishonesty is not attractive to God.

Lying lips are an abomination to the LORD, but those who deal truthfully are His delight. (Proverbs 12:22)

Finally, God is attracted to those who practice honor. Malachi 1:6 says we are to honor God because He is our Father. Exodus 20:12

tells us to honor our parents so that we will have long life. And when it comes to releasing a multigenerational anointing, honor is key. Honor releases blessing!

HONORING THE FORMER

Jesus epitomized honor. While men reached for thrones to build their own kingdoms, Jesus reached for a towel to wash men's feet. Just as God is calling the older generations to believe in, inspire, and empower the younger, He is calling the younger to honor the older. In God's plan, honor releases blessing.

In 2001, our ministry honored several key leaders in the city with the Golden Towel awards, given to individuals who had been tangible expressions of Christ. One of the recipients was Dodie Osteen, widow of the late John Osteen of Houston's Lakewood Church. When I was young and new in the ministry, Brother Osteen and Dodie were personal encouragements to me and always made me feel welcome. Dodie still tells people that she thinks of me as a son. I wanted, in this small way, to express my honor to her not only for the inspiration she and Brother Osteen were to me but to recognize all that they had done for so many others.

So a few years later, in 2005, the River Oaks chapter of Women's Aglow in Houston invited me to speak at their annual Christmas banquet. I serve on their advisory board, but I did not know they were planning to honor me that day for my service and for being, in their eyes, a father to the city. Dodie had been asked to introduce me and to present the gifts they selected for me: a beautiful small treasure chest filled with the same gems that are on the Levitical ephod and a white linen towel, signifying the servanthood of Christ. Because I have trouble seeing myself as a spiritual father, I was humbled that these ladies—especially Dodie, a spiritual mother in our city—would honor me that way. Years earlier, we had chosen to honor her, and now she was blessing me.

A few days earlier, I had been honored in a similar fashion by José and Magda Hermida. Magda ministers to the Hispanic community in Houston and throughout South America through her radio program.

They had invited me to speak at their annual Christmas breakfast, with an audience of over one thousand ladies and ministry leaders. Before I'd started speaking, they'd honored me with a plaque that read,

> We honor you as a father, covering, and inspiration, not only to us but to those you encounter wherever you go. We love you and appreciate your love and concern for us all.

José and Magda choose to honor me as a father—though they are several years older than me and are considered a father and mother to so many people—and I desire to bless them, as well. Therefore, I am committed to letting them share in my inheritance by supporting their ministry any way I can.

Other ministries in Houston honor us for paving the path for their ministries. Some work in the inner city where we first began our own ministry. Because they honor us, we bless them and invest our time, facilities, and resources in them.

When you honor a person, you endear yourself to him or her, and he or she will probably want to bless you in return. The older generations have an inheritance to pass on to the younger; but inheritance is received, not taken. The younger must be willing to honor the older to receive an inheritance.

During one of our Compassion Coalition pastors and leaders meetings, we honored three fathers in our city who had each been serving in ministry for over fifty years. They were Bishop Roy Lee Kossie of Latter Day Deliverance Revival Church in Houston's inner city; Pastor Cantu, who leads Hispanic church El Tabernaculo Asambleas de Dios; and Pastor Fahed Karmout of Arabic Evangelical Church.

The older generations have an inheritance to pass on to the younger; but inheritance is received, not taken. The younger must be willing to honor the older to receive an inheritance.

The audience included over one hundred pastors and leaders from all different denominations and ministries. During an extended prayer time at the end of the meeting, each person had the opportunity to receive a father's blessing from each these leaders. I was impressed with the genuine diversity and the beautiful dynamics of the day as we witnessed a multigenerational and multiethnic group honor these spiritual fathers who were all finishing their races well. We lingered in the presence of God, His anointing so powerful and so evident that many would comment on it afterward. Pastor and Mrs. Karmout even said that it reminded them of the revival in Jerusalem in the 1970s. Because we honored those who have gone before us, God blessed our time together.

A generation that recognizes the importance of honoring the former and does so will encourage the former to bless them in return, which will result in a corporate multigenerational anointing.

"COME WITH US"

Many in the emerging generation recognize that they need the wisdom and experience of the former generations. They may have a different way of presentation, a different style of music—a different style of everything—but they know they can't completely disregard the ways of the former generation. The only way to cross over into the promised land of blessing and destiny is to recognize and honor the former and say, "Give us your blessing and join with us."

Second Kings 6 reports how the sons of the prophets came to Elisha, the older prophet who had received a double portion from his spiritual father, Elijah. The place they lived was not big enough, and so they asked for his blessing and his permission to build elsewhere. To me, this is an analogy of the younger generation coming to the older and saying, "What we're doing is unique, and what we desire to do is different. But we recognize we need your blessing."

Elisha gave them his blessing, and then they asked for more—they asked him to accompany them on their journey. There is no mention of him actually finding and building a place for them, but he was present on the journey. The younger prophets didn't need him to do the work because they knew what to do.

The same is true in the emerging generation. They are full of vision as a prophetic generation. They will fulfill the dreams of the previous generations. And if they recognize that they need the wisdom and covering of those who have gone before them, they will be unstoppable!

The sons of the prophets felt strengthened just by Elisha's presence. Later, when they lost their ax head—which represented their passion, edge, direction, and strength—they approached Elisha, who said to them, quite simply, "Take me back to where you lost it." (See 2 Kings 6:6.)

Likewise, today, those who have been around awhile and have experienced the hard times of ministry can help others rediscover their passion and zeal. They can help them return to their first love.

How does this happen? By directing those who have been discouraged by life to go back to where they lost their passion and zeal—where they were disappointed, where they were disillusioned by leaders, where they turned their focus from God to man—to confront their hurt and rediscover their passion and zeal. After all, what is lost can be found only where a person lost it.

Those who have been around awhile and have experienced the hard times of ministry can help others rediscover their passion and zeal. They can help them return to their first love.

The former generations have to bless the emerging generation, and the emerging generation has to honor the former generations. If we all work together, we can accomplish mighty exploits for God.

We've seen the former rain, and we've glimpsed the latter rain; but when the former and latter rains come together, the floodgates will open and release the rivers of God.

THE PRINCIPLE AT WORK IN MY OWN LIFE

In the early 1980s, when I was introduced to Dr. Cole's ministry, his message of consecration gripped my heart and connected with my spirit. In 1983, I began volunteering in one of his temporary Houston offices, which was the headquarters for a Christian men's event scheduled for April of the following year.

When a Christian businessman invited me to join him at a meeting so I could meet Dr. Cole, I was hesitant but decided to go anyway. I respected Dr. Cole's position but did not want to pursue him. However, in the middle of the meeting, Dr. Cole pulled me aside and said that he had heard about my work, and asked how much it would cost him to hire me to be the National Young Adult Coordinator for the 1984 event.

"Dr. Cole, I'm not a hireling," I said. "I'm already serving full time, and I will continue to do so because I believe in your message. I appreciate the offer, but God is my source, and I feel that the Lord has challenged me to serve you for this event because of its significance and the impact it will have on the men in our nation."

I served Dr. Cole not only for that event but for years to come, and he became like a spiritual father to me. I didn't pursue him for what he could do for me, but God validated me through him as he invested both his time and character in me. I didn't necessarily spend a lot of time with him, but what time I did spend with him was quality.

As years went by, people would tell me the kind things Dr. Cole said about me. I realized that I was receiving an inheritance from him, not because I asked for one, but because I served him in honor.

Honor released blessing. Once, Dr. Cole was ministering in another country, and someone told him how I quoted him all the time. He responded by saying that I didn't have to quote him, because all the things he had taught me were now mine. What I learned from Dr. Cole had become my inheritance, part of my DNA.

When my real father and stepfather died, they both left me golf clubs—and I don't even golf! But when Dr. Cole died, I received something very valuable. When he first started out in ministry, he'd prayed in an old church late at night to prepare for the next day's service. He'd put a blanket over his shoulders to keep himself warm. Often, his kids had slept on the pews next to him while he prayed so they could be close to him, and he'd put blankets on them, as well. When his ministry had grown and he'd begun traveling, he would take the bedspread from the hotel room and put it over his shoulders before he prayed—a habit that had become part of his prayer life.

Years ago, someone had made him a handmade prayer blanket. I can only imagine the hundreds or even thousands of tears that had been shed and the countless of hours of prayer that had taken place under that blanket, and when he died, he'd left it to me. Because of the honor I'd given him over the years, he wanted to bless me. It is a gift I treasure because it represents what Dr. Cole's life was all about. It is a reminder to me of all the times I heard him pray, even when he was physically exhausted from ministering, "God, give me a little more time to reach a few more men, a few more families." What I received from serving Dr. Cole is an inheritance that will take me far beyond the riches of gold or silver.

I was also blessed to have a relationship with another mighty man of God, Leonard Ravenhill. I didn't pursue him, either; we just happened to connect. He had come across a prepublished book I wrote in 1990 and had begun to peruse it. Something about the book engaged his heart, and so he began writing notes to me and praying for me.

Eventually, I got to meet him and visit with him from time to time. I came to think of him as a spiritual grandfather. Sometimes, I would feel impelled to call him, and he would say, "Oh, dear Brother Doug, I was just praying for you." I was so humbled that someone so important in the kingdom of God would take time to pray for me.

Before Brother Ravenhill died, he was in a semi-comatose state. One day, I called his wife, Martha, to see how he was doing. She began telling me how people from all over the world were coming to see him, and some of them would actually take his hand and place it on their forehead, expecting to get a double portion of his anointing.

In the same manner, sometimes people try to coerce me into becoming a spiritual father to them to receive a blessing. But relationships don't work that way, and passing on an inheritance doesn't work that way. Inheritances cannot be taken; they are earned by taking on the character and spirit of the message and the messenger. You can't just take it; it is mutually given and received.

I was in an airport when I got the call from Susie at my office that Brother Ravenhill had passed away, so I immediately rerouted my flight so that I could attend his funeral. On the way there, I was contemplating his life and the many people with whom he had relationship— people like David Wilkerson, the late Keith Green, and Jacob Aranza. Suddenly, I doubted my own relationship with him. A voice in my head seemed to say, *Who do you think you are, imagining that he is really your spiritual grandfather? Yes, you did spend time with him, and you had a relationship with him, but he was such an important man. Did he really see you that way?*

I attended the funeral, then went to the burial. Here was this great man of God being buried in an obscure cemetery outside a small rural town in East Texas. It so typified the humility of his life. While I was there, God Himself began dispelling the doubts I had about my relationship with him as various people came up to me and asked, "Are you Doug Stringer?" They began telling me how Brother Ravenhill always spoke so highly of me and how he recommended my book to them.

Suddenly, it didn't matter how much time I'd spent with him. What mattered was that, without even trying, I had received a spiritually rich inheritance from him. Because I had honored him, he had blessed me. Today, I have also gained the blessing of a friendship with Leonard's son, David, who carries on his father's passion for prayer, worship, and living wholly for God. In fact it was my great honor to be asked to endorse books by both David and his wife, Nancy.

A LOST ART

In many cultures of the world, honor is still a way of life, especially when it comes to honoring previous generations. It is not considered unusual for parents and grandparents to be cared for in their latter years in the homes of their children and grandchildren. Instead of the elderly being a burden, they are viewed as a blessing, a vast resource of wisdom and knowledge. Even in America, there once was a time when we took pains to honor the elderly, recognizing them for their faithfulness and wisdom. The younger generations appreciated the experience and insights of their elders.

I was reminded of my own heritage of honor when I watched the movie *The Last Samurai*. The Japanese word samurai simply means "servant." The entire duty of a samurai was to serve the emperor and defend his honor.

After my mother became a widow, my sister and brother both asked her to live with them, but she wouldn't have it. "I live with my oldest boy, Dougie!" I was thirty-eight years old, single, and leading an international ministry—buying a house with my mother was not exactly the path I had envisioned for my life at that time! But as the oldest Asian son, I knew it was my responsibility to care for her. In 1996, she moved in with me and lived with me for nearly eight years until she moved to Austin to be near my sister.

She had begun having some health problems, and I was traveling a lot. A year and a half later, she went to be with Jesus, just a few weeks after she had been diagnosed with cancer. Now, I wouldn't trade those eight years together for anything in the world. I am so thankful I chose to honor her that way.

I still find myself honoring my mother by obeying certain things she taught me, such as taking off my shoes before going into the house. Anytime I determine to walk through the house fully shod, I can get only so far before I hear her voice saying, "Dougie! Do you have your shoes on? Douglas, take off your shoes!" Now I even make my guests take off their shoes!

I also remember my mother telling me not to throw tissues in the toilet. "Dougie, they clog the drain!" I would argue with her that there was no difference between tissues and toilet paper. Years later, I learned that she was right when I saw it on television. It was confirmed again by a woman who had heard me tell the story when I was preaching at a church in Cheshire, Connecticut. She sent me an e-mail entitled "Your Mother Was Right":

> I heard you tell the story about your mother and her opposition to having tissues thrown into the toilet. She was right, you know! I laughed to myself as I thought what my nine-year-old would tell you if you were to walk up and ask him why we don't throw tissues into the toilet.
>
> A couple of years ago, Chaska and I set up a small experiment. We put a tissue in a cup of water and toilet paper in another cup of water and let it sit overnight. Sure enough, the next day, the toilet paper had broken up very well, but the tissue was still completely intact.
>
> While I was talking with my husband about what you had said, I looked at Chaska and asked, "Chaska, why don't we throw tissues into the toilet?"
>
> He looked up at me over the rim of his glasses and said, "Because they'll clog the drain."
>
> Then, knowing that our six-year-old had been trained not to throw the tissues into the toilet, I asked, "Kenya, why don't we throw tissues into the toilet?"
>
> He raised his curly mop and said, "Because we frow dem in the trash."
>
> "But, Kenya, why do we throw them in the trash?"
>
> "Because we can't frow dem in the toiwet."
>
> "Kenya, what would happen if we threw them in the toilet?"
>
> He raised his curly mop again and paused for a moment. Then, making a gagging noise and sticking out his precious little tongue, he said, "It would choke!"

HONOR GUARDS FOR GOD

Unfortunately, it seems this type of honor for previous generations is becoming a lost art. We have neither learned nor passed on the principles of honor in our homes, much less in our schools and workplaces. And if we did not learn to honor our parents—for some of us, because our parents were absent—how will we ever learn to honor our God?

Our ministry hosted a meeting for our Disaster Preparedness and Response network in Washington, DC, with ministry leaders from around the nation with whom we had partnered for relief efforts for Hurricanes Katrina and Rita. One of our guests, Pastor Charles Burchett from Kirbyville, Texas, and Somebody Cares Jasper/Newton Counties, spent some of his free time visiting Arlington Cemetery. He had previously preached a sermon on the changing of the guards at the Tomb of the Unknown Soldier and now, seeing it in person, he was deeply touched by the display of honor. According to Pastor Burchett:

> The tomb is guarded twenty-four hours a day, 365 days a year, by specially trained members of the 3rd United States Infantry Regiment. This select group of sentinels is called the Honor Guard....Being selected to stand watch over the graves of the Unknown Soldiers is one of the highest honors a soldier in the United States Army can be granted.
>
> Day or night, and regardless of the elements, the tomb is guarded, and has been guarded every minute of every day since 1937. The sentinels never show signs of being too cold or hot, and they never change the way they guard the tomb, even at night when there is no one watching. They do what they do for the ones they are honoring, not for spectators or for their own personal advancement. They genuinely believe that the Unknown Soldiers deserve the very best that they have to give.

Pastor Burchett challenges us to show the same kind of dedication to God the Father.

Twenty-four hours a day and 365 days a year, the Lord God Almighty sits in the center of heaven. He invites men and women to receive the highest of all honors in the kingdom of God, that of coming into His presence. The disciplines of holiness and honor require wholeheartedness, dignity, perseverance, diligence, praise, humility, reverence, respect, and vigilance. Without these characteristics, no one can stand before the Lord.

Honor releases blessing. First, we are to honor God. We are to honor His Word, His person, and His character, so we can walk in His blessing and favor. We honor Him by practicing godly characteristics and principles and by exhibiting the character of Christ. We honor Him by giving our time and resources to His work.

Second, we are to honor our parents. Even though we may not always agree with them, we can show respect and honor even when we disagree. Honoring our parents is the first commandment to come with a promise, the blessing of long life. (See Deuteronomy 5:16.)

Third, we are told to honor the spiritual authorities God has placed in our lives. Again, even if we don't agree with them, we must still respect their office and the fact that God has appointed them. We remember that they are human and flawed, but we serve as unto God, and therefore, we honor them. (See Ephesians 6:7.)

Fourth, we honor one another: spouses, family, friends, coworkers, and so forth.

And last, we honor former generations. It would benefit us greatly to study the origins of some of our favorite hymns and read about the spiritual giants who have gone before us, those sold-out pioneers in the faith who paved the way for our ministries on the earth.

Wisdom doesn't come solely from our successes but from our failures. The wisdom of the elders was often obtained by learning from their mistakes. Honoring those who have gone before us can save us from making the same mistakes. It can be liberating for us.

As we honor God, our natural and spiritual parents, our authorities, those who have gone before us, and one another, we position ourselves to hear the wonderful words from our Father "Well done!" "That's my girl!" "That's my boy!"

9

RAISING A STANDARD OF RIGHTEOUSNESS

In 2004, I was invited on a ministry trip to Brazil, a country with more than 206 million people.[22] I was told that 12 million of them are homeless teenagers and children, and, according to The World Bank, nearly 10 percent of the population lives in poverty.[23]

While there, I was asked to speak to a group of youth leaders. I arrived to a church packed with several thousand young people and their leaders, filling all the seats and even standing outside. I was moved by the energy and excitement of this generation, by such hunger and passion in the midst of despair. The very facet of Brazilian society that is under oppression is the one that is rising up and setting the standard!

All over the world, God is calling forth a generation endued with power to raise a standard of passion, purity, and purpose. They are young people who do not focus on the circumstances; instead, they look at the promises of God and say, "In the midst of impossibility, we see a God of possibility."

All over the world, God is calling forth a generation endued with power to raise a standard of passion, purity, and purpose.

---

22. "Brazil," The World Bank, http://data.worldbank.org/country/brazil.
23. Ibid.

In one Christian country, a pastor was arrested for speaking out on moral issues, including homosexuality while teaching on Romans 1. And in another nation where I preach, opposers of the gospel are trying to change legislation to be more antagonistic toward the church. This is becoming increasingly true in America, as well. We have free speech until it goes countercultural and contradicts the mores of our society.

What have we come to? We're witnessing the "de-Christ-ing" of a generation. As a nation, we've lowered the standard, and it's time for every generation to raise that standard once again and say, "We will not be moved; we're going to fight a battle, and we're willing to die for it."

Many voices of compromise are out there, but the Bible is our standard of truth. God's Word must be our own standard. We must raise it up and follow after God with our whole hearts.

WHAT IS A STANDARD?

Historically, a standard, or a flag, served three purposes:

1. To identify a national or tribal group

2. To claim possession of a space or territory

3. To mark a festivity or celebration

Each of the twelve tribes of Israel had a standard that identified its tribe in camp and in battle. In battle, a standard is used to identify the regiment or platoon and to communicate a variety of messages, including nationality and instructions to advance or retreat.

A standard is also a banner, and God's banner over us is love. (See Song of Solomon 2:4.) Jesus has already set a standard over us and is calling us to raise that same standard of life, love, and purpose for others to follow in the dark world. It's a standard of hope! A generation that raises the standard of God and does not lower it will inspire the rest of their generation to follow.

God is calling all generations to set a standard and collectively fulfill it. Isaiah 49:22–23 says,

Thus says the Lord God: "Behold, I will lift My hand in an oath to the nations, and set up My standard for the peoples; they shall bring your sons in their arms, and your daughters shall be carried on their shoulders; kings shall be your foster fathers, and their queens your nursing mothers; they shall bow down to you with their faces to the earth, and lick up the dust of your feet. Then you will know that I am the Lord, for they shall not be ashamed who wait for Me."

What a wonderful promise! Whatever is going on around us, even in the midst of raging battles, God says He will be a banner and will set a standard for His people.

It's time to claim our territory—our families, our churches, our cities, our nation, and this emerging generation—for God. And God wants us to celebrate Him for our victories. He's called us to be like the leper who returned to thank Jesus for his healing. God wants us to have an attitude of gratitude no matter what we may be going through.

CHARACTERISTICS OF A STANDARD-BEARER

I believe God is calling people of the emerging generation to be standard-bearers who say, "We will not be moved." Those who bear a standard are those who cast a vision and raise it high for others to follow. They not only raise a standard; they raise a standard based on the Word of God. A standard of character is what attracts the very power and presence of God, empowering standard-bearers to be leaders in this generation. What kind of leaders is God looking for?

First, God is looking for leaders of humility, holiness, honor, and honesty. These are individuals willing to walk in the fear of the Lord and a spirit of brokenness. (See Psalm 51:17.) Proverbs 22:4 says, *"By humility and the fear of the Lord are riches and honor and life."* Only the presence of God can bring personal and corporate transformation. We need standard-bearers who will walk in the attributes that attract God's presence and favor.

The book of Esther is a beautiful story of how just one moment of favor from the king turned around a whole national disaster. In the same way, one moment of favor from the King of Kings and Lord of Lords can instantly turn our circumstances around. God can do in a moment what it takes years for us to do on our own.

Second, God wants to raise up leaders with a strong personal prayer life. Our public lives are determined by what we do behind closed doors when no one else can see us. Do we exhibit the power of God or the lack of it? Who are we in private?

Standard-bearers are called to a higher consecration. The high calling of God is not about men ordaining us but about God setting us apart. Ordination is about men recognizing what God has already done, and with that recognition comes greater responsibility. "Though others may, we may not." God is calling us to judge ourselves by a higher standard. A strong prayer life and being the same person of consecration and holiness in private as we are in public are God's desires for His standard-bearers.

Third, God wants leaders with a kingdom vision who can see things beyond themselves. Life is not about personal feelings; it's about the bigger picture. Leaders don't have time to get caught up in what is going on around them, because their battle is not with flesh and blood. (See Ephesians 6:12.) We need something real and tangible inside of us to keep us going. We cannot live on momentum alone, because momentum eventually runs out. Passion without principles and purpose will not sustain us.

Fourth, God is looking for leaders of perseverance, who keep focused on the vision with persistence and courage. When we get discouraged, we can compromise God's intended purposes and vision for our lives. We need to remind ourselves of the promises of God, especially when we go through challenges, because holding on to His prophetic promise keeps us focused on our purposes and our destinations. We cannot allow ourselves to be distracted by our challenges. As Dr. Cole used to say, "Winners only see where they're going, not what they're going through."

We need something real and tangible inside of us to keep us going. We cannot live on momentum alone, because momentum eventually runs out. Passion without principles and purpose will not sustain us.

We need to be like Joshua and Caleb, who looked past their circumstances. The other ten spies came back reporting, "It is as God says it is—but the giants were so big that we're like grasshoppers in their sight." (See Numbers 13:33.) If we see ourselves as grasshoppers, so will the giants.

On the other hand, Joshua and Caleb were able to see the finish line and hold on to the promises of God. God has given us prophetic words so we will not lose sight of our destiny, regardless of what we see. He has already given us a promise of victory and not of defeat. God says to raise a standard, and He will empower us to fight and win!

When we abide in God's holiness, nothing can come against us. He is our banner and rallying point, our victory. It's not about what we see; it's about who we know and who lives in us!

TRUE WORSHIPPERS

There is one more crucial way to attract God's favor—by worshipping Him in spirit and in truth. (See John 4:24.) Worship is the foundation that attracts the manifest presence of the Lord.

When we are in God's presence, in that holy and consecrated place, our communion with Him is completely undivided. We are so taken with God's power that all we can say is, "Holy, holy, holy is the name of God!" (See Isaiah 6:3.) We are in awe of God. In that place, we see we are undone and we recognize His abounding grace. In undivided worship, we receive our commission to go out with His authority. (See Isaiah 6:5–9.) Our gifts and abilities can take us only so far, but God can take us places that seem impossible.

COURAGE BEGETS COURAGE

In the movie *The Patriot*, the minutemen were running away from the British Army in fear. Their standard, the American flag, had been dropped to the ground. In a moment of personal courage, Mel Gibson's character grabbed the flag in the midst of the retreating army and waved it proudly as he advanced toward the enemy. That one act of courage brought hope and strength to the other soldiers as they, too, faced the enemy, reminding them they were part of a battle and destiny much bigger than themselves.

Likewise, in the Battle of Iwo Jima, amid the bullets and the carnage, five American marines and one navy corpsman grabbed the American flag, raised it, and staked it into the ground as if to say, "We will not be defeated!" The moment was immortalized in a Pulitzer-Prize-winning photograph that speaks a thousand words of courage and inspiration to us even today.

In the same way, this emerging generation will lead a movement of purity, passion, and purpose in the name of the Lord. They are a generation unashamed of the gospel and are unwilling to compromise the true standard, the Word of God. It's a standard they are willing to raise high for all to see. They send forth the message "We will not be moved." And as they live the standard, they attract the manifest presence of God and are endued with His power. As they move forth in courage, others are encouraged and inspired to persevere in the battle.

WHO WILL GO?

God is urgently calling His standard-bearers to assemble and lead the generations into their prophetic destinies. So how can we be part of the high-standard movement? How can we be leaders with courage to fight? How can we participate in a generation-spanning movement, culminating in the fulfillment of the words and prayers spoken by the prophets of old?

We must walk in humility, holiness, honor, and honesty in God's presence through intimate prayer, praise, and worship. We must have persevering and courageous hearts to uphold those standards no matter what giants or circumstances stand in our way. And we must live beyond ourselves and become part of a bigger vision.

Who among us will raise that standard and be a standard-bearer, doing whatever it takes to attract the favor and presence of God? Who will walk forth endued with power from the Source and Giver? As John Wesley, the great revivalist of the eighteenth century, said, "Give me one hundred men who fear nothing but God, and are determined to know nothing among men but Christ and him crucified, and I will set the world on fire."[24]

Are you ready to be part of a multigenerational movement that raises a standard and changes the world? We have all heard it said that you can lead a horse to water, but you can't make him drink. This may be true, but you can give the horse enough salt to make him thirsty. If we truly are the salt of the earth, as God has called us to be, we will create thirst in those around us.

> *Then the men of the city said to Elisha, "Please notice, the situation of this city is pleasant, as my lord sees; but the water is bad, and the ground barren." And he said, "Bring me a new bowl, and put salt in it." So they brought it to him. Then he went out to the source of the water, and cast in the salt there, and said, "Thus says the LORD: 'I have healed this water; from it there shall be no more death or barrenness.'"* (2 Kings 2:19–21)

In this story, the water in the land was bitter and poisonous and people were dying from it. But when Elisha put salt in the source, the water was cleansed and the barrenness left.

SALTY CHRISTIANS

Salt is both a seasoning and a preservative, and it also has medicinal values. Likewise, this emerging generation has learned to be the salt of the earth, bringing healing, life, and flavor to a world of barrenness and

---

24. Gerard Benjamin Fleet Hallock, *The Evangelistic Cyclopedia: A New Century Handbook of Evangelism* (New York: George H. Doran Company, 1922), 165.

death. Like salt, they can tenderize and soften hearts that are hardened to the gospel.

In spite of their pasts, the words spoken against them, circumstances that have crushed them, and prejudices raised against them, "salty" Christians hold fast to God's true revelation of their identity in Him. Furthermore, a generation that knows how to forgive and even honor those who have hurt them will experience freedom in their futures and will become the salt of the earth. They will be a generation that will make others thirsty for God; and those who are hungry and thirsty for righteousness will be filled! (See Matthew 5:6.)

A generation that knows how to forgive and even honor those who have hurt them will experience freedom in their futures and will become the salt of the earth.

GOD IS GIVING US A WAKE-UP CALL

You and I have a great opportunity, even a responsibility, to influence this emerging generation with the gospel and to guide them out of the wilderness. Time is running out, and there is a sense of urgency in the spiritual realm.

I once had a sobering dream that God used to illustrate this urgency to me. In the dream, I was staying in a hotel and had an urgent meeting at 7:00 the next morning. The Lord showed me in advance that this meeting was very critical. If I made the meeting and spoke the word of the Lord into the situation, multitudes would be spared some tragedy. If I missed the appointment and the word of the Lord was not spoken in due time, multitudes would be in danger. I took this very seriously.

I called the front desk and requested a 5:30 AM wake-up call, allowing me plenty of time to make the meeting. And to ensure I would be on time, I used my standard backup plan and set my alarm clock to ring a few minutes after the wake-up call. At 5:30 AM, the phone rang.

"Mr. Stringer, this is your wake-up call."

I said thank you and hung up the phone. I thought, *I have a few more minutes before the alarm clock rings. I'm going back to sleep; I'm exhausted.* I lay back down.

Then the alarm clock rang. I was still tired, so I pushed the snooze button, thinking, *Just a few more minutes, and I'll be ready to get up.*

The alarm rang again, and I pushed the snooze button again—I did this several times. When I finally woke up, it was after 7 AM!

The Lord spoke to my heart in the dream and said, "Because you missed that meeting, multitudes are now in danger. You didn't speak the word in season at that meeting, and now you are responsible."

I woke up with a soberness and fear of the Lord. I recognized the potential we have in this season to kick-start a revival. But for that to happen, we have to awake from our sleep. We cannot be distracted. We cannot look to the left or to the right. We must fine-tune our ears and hear what the Spirit of the Lord is saying. God is giving us a wake-up call. He wants us to arise! He wants to bring a sustainable, exponential awakening that transcends every denomination and ethnicity. This move of God will bridge the generations. The anointing of the older generation will be poured out exponentially on the younger generation.

In the midst of worldwide turmoil and shaking, an army of young people is being released. Many will emerge as full-time volunteer laborers for God's kingdom. (See Psalm 110:2–3.) They are determined to make a difference. God will enable them to affect every element of their culture and subculture.

You and I have a strategic role to play in this process. Each generation has something to give. The wisdom of the older joined with the zeal and passion of youth will affect many with the gospel.

God's intention is to bring revival in an exponential way through a young generation, and we are to stand with them. What we do together is critical. God intends to release a massive move of His Spirit, and He is calling the bride to prepare herself and restore the altar of worship for the ark of His presence. When all that can be shaken has been shaken,

God wants His church to be an ark of refuge, a place to which people can run.

The ark of God's presence will rest in the church that has prepared herself, the one that has been diligent and is spotless and blameless. She will not be a cosmetic bride, compensating on the outside for lack on the inside. Nor will she become a lifeless institution. With depth of character, she will be prepared for the Lord's presence. There, God will dwell.

ON THE EDGE OF ETERNITY

Satan failed to accomplish his task when he killed the innocent children in Moses' and Jesus' day. Now he is targeting this emerging prophetic generation. He wants to stop them early on so they won't fulfill their purpose. What can you and I do to help?

It's time for the children to come forth, and we must give them strength. It's time for the church's rebirth, and we must persevere through the delivery!

God's intended purpose is to bring a great awakening to and through this generation. We must awaken from slumber and heed the Lord's call for our nation and the world in this crucial hour.

The bottom line is this: God is doing something! We don't need to fear what is happening but embrace it and take it one bit at a time. We must be willing to go with the change. We need one another; we simply cannot do it alone. There is a treasure in this generation, and we must find it.

At this very moment, millions are in the crucial valley of decision, living on the edge of eternity. We are responsible for bringing them through the valley and to the cross. The time is now!

PART 3

MY DADDY ROCKS!

10

THE ROCK OF ALL AGES

Returning from a ministry trip to Fiji, I stopped in Denver for a few days. At the airport, I saw a father with his young son, who was wearing a T-shirt that read, "My daddy rocks!"

At that tender age, this child's world revolved around his daddy. I was reminded of myself at that age and how my trust in my father had been severed. I wondered how long it would last for that little boy. As the years go on, would this dad provide the acceptance, approval, and affirmation his son will need? Will he be able to withstand the storms of life, allowing his son to grow up feeling safe, secure, and protected? Will this son be able to stand on the trust and intimacy he experienced with his dad, or will his dad respond to the cares of this world in such a way that, instead, would rock this little boy's world?

I thought of James Boswell, who wrote a biography on the great British author Samuel Johnson. (The story is sometimes attributed to Johnson's life but, nonetheless, it is a stirring story with a profound point.) As a boy, James Boswell spent the day fishing with his father. His father was an influential and busy man, so this day of intentional attention spoke volumes to the young boy. Years later, someone came across his father's journal after his death and discovered that his father's perception of that day had been very different from his own. He wrote, "Gone fishing today with my son; a day wasted."[25]

What an impact a father's love has on a child's life, and how devastating when it is lacking! What hurt it brings to a child's tender heart when his father has no time him. How difficult it is when a child discovers that his father's perception of their relationship is so very different from his own. This discovery can become a turning point for a child. He will either continue to say, "My daddy rocks," or the reality of a severed relationship will rock his very foundation.

After the father of Ruben, a spiritual son in the ministry, was killed when he was five years old. Ruben carried a deep wound within him, which manifested in his behavior because of his brokenness and hurt. After Ruben came to the Lord, he became a part of our ministry, where he came to know the healing power of his heavenly Father.

Years later, I entrusted Ruben with a challenging project of overseeing a citywide outreach event with several major athletes, businessmen, ministry leaders, and even Hollywood producers. His responsibilities included meeting with pastors and leaders from local schools, representing the ministry at meetings of business leaders, identifying children from needy families with vision and hearing problems, and coordinating a number of volunteers to box up food for the families. He was also involved in media interviews and other critical tasks.

The event culminated with the national premier of a Hollywood movie at a Houston theater. During the evening, Ruben's then twenty-one-year-old son, Chris, had the opportunity to introduce himself to some of the business and ministry leaders his dad had been working with. "My name is Chris. I'm Ruben's son," he said proudly. Many people spoke, attesting to how much they appreciated Ruben, what a great job he had done with the outreach, and how well he represented Somebody Cares.

Later, as Chris looked around and considered all that had occurred—hundreds of children receiving new hearing aids and/or eyeglasses walking down a red carpet like celebrities; families getting free

25. Kenneth D. Boa, *Conformed to His Image: Biblical and Practical Approaches to Spiritual Formation* (Grand Rapids, MI: Zondervan, 2001), 247.

groceries; television cameras and newspaper reporters recording all that had happened—he said to his mother, "You know what? My dad rocks!"

Even after years of watching his family go through life's struggles, trials, and difficulties, this grown son—now a husband and a father—can still say, "My dad rocks!" His dad received healing from his heavenly Father through the Spirit of adoption and was able to secure his family on the one true Foundation, which is the Rock, Jesus Christ. Today, Ruben runs his own successful family-owned business.

THE GEN-EDGE MIRACLE

Jesus is the Rock of all Ages, and His Father—our heavenly Father—is the Father of all generations. He is a multigenerational God. He desires to bridge all generations, utilizing the strengths of each and linking them with a common purpose. Once each generation is sanctified and brought together with the other generations, the result will be a force to be reckoned with. It will fan the flames for revival like we've never ever seen.

The Bible says, *"Your old men shall dream dreams, your young men shall see visions"* (Joel 2:28; see also Acts 2:17). The inference is that the older generation has dreams yet to be fulfilled, but they will not be fulfilled until the passion, zeal, and vision of a younger generation are applied to them. On the other hand, the younger generation needs the wisdom and dreams of the older generation to accomplish their destinies.

In Scripture, King David dreamed to build a glorious temple, a house for God. His desire was good, but God said that the temple would be built by his son Solomon. Knowing his son would be young and inexperienced, David began laying out the plans God had placed on his own heart so that his son would have something by which to build. Solomon entered into the labor of the temple with his father's blessing and wisdom.

In May 2006, I was invited to Australia by one of my sons in the faith, Andrew Merry, and a group of pastors. I was to preach two weeks of revival services in the Geelong area of the Bellarine Peninsula. In 1983, I had picked up Andrew while he was hitchhiking through Houston. Through a series of divine "mishaps," Andrew had stayed in my home and came to know Jesus as his Savior. He had gone on to pastor a significant Baptist church in the area, and he considers me a spiritual father.

The pastors who invited me were from various denominations in the region and had fasted for forty days before my arrival. I had met some of them the first time I visited Australia twenty years earlier. During one of the meetings for pastors and leaders, some of them shared how they had come to know the Lord through our ministry, and others said that they looked to me as a spiritual covering. A few years earlier, during another visit, some of them had said that they saw me as a Charles Finney in the area. Although I don't see myself that way, I've been very humbled and encouraged by them. It has been one of my prayers since the beginning of the ministry to have a passion and anointing like Charles Finney's, to impact the community and see people stay true to their Father.

As I was concluding one of the revival services at Ocean Grove Fellowship, I called forward all the pastors, leaders, ministry workers, and elders I had met on my trips throughout the years, and I had them face the audience. Then I looked out at the spectators and said, "Behold your fathers and mothers."

Then I addressed my fellow ministry workers, the "young people" of twenty years ago, as they looked out at this awesome group of young people, the "dreamers" of Joel 2 and Acts 2: "Behold your sons and daughters."

As they stood face-to-face, generation-to-generation, I continued, "Think of all those years ago, when you were full of passion and zeal and nothing could stop you! Then you hit challenges. Today, you feel the physical and emotional wear and tear, the setbacks, the disappointments, the broken and shattered dreams.

"Maybe you feel as if you've failed or that your life has been in vain. But look! Your life has not been in vain! Behold this emerging generation of visionaries, full of zeal and passion and uniqueness! This is what you've labored for!

"Your dreams shall be accomplished and fulfilled through this new generation of prophets and prophetesses! You didn't fail, and your dreams have not died—they're still alive! They will be accomplished. Be encouraged with the passion and zeal of the youth and their uniqueness. Come alongside them and give strength and wisdom to deliver."

To the visionaries, the young people, I said, "You're not alone. We recognize your uniqueness, and we are here to cover you and give you strength to come forth into your destinies!"

It was a powerful demonstration of the multigenerational blessing God wants to impart to His people. The emerging generation realized their need of the former, and the former generation was able to shift their focus from their own journeys to the emerging generation, giving them hope and expectation that their dreams would yet be fulfilled. Hallelujah!

11

THE FATHER OF
ALL NATIONS

"You said, 'Ask and I'll give the nations to you";
O Lord, that's the cry of my heart;
Distant shores and the islands will see
Your light, as it rises on us;
O Lord, I ask for the nations."[26]
—*Reuben Morgan*

I get choked up each time I hear this song by Hillsong of Australia, quoting the prayer of David in Psalm 2:8:

Ask of Me, and I will give You the nations for Your inheritance, and the ends of the earth for Your possession.

I believe this is a cry of our generations— a promise of God that He will give us the nations, because He is the Father of all nations. All we have to do is ask.

My friend Suliasi invited me to minister in Fiji for the first time in 1993. At that time, he was director of Every Home for Christ Fiji, a group of passionate young people committed to taking the gospel to every single home in Fiji. Their plan was to do it not just once but three

---

26. Reuben Morgan, "You Said," 1998.

times. Some even made vows not to marry until they had accomplished the mission. People thought they were crazy, but they did it, and God has honored them for their faithfulness.

Today, Suliasi pastors one of the largest churches in the Southern Hemisphere. It's located in Suva, Fiji. When I go there and see the flags from every nation displayed throughout the sanctuary, I am reminded that God is the Father of all nations and all generations. Suliasi's mission has never changed; his desire is to reach the nations, and his passion is the Great Commission. After all these years, the cry of his heart remains, "Lord, give me the nations!"

That has become the cry of his brothers and sisters in the church movement, as well. Because of the seeds Suliasi and others have planted over the years, Fiji has been dramatically transformed by the hand of God.

You can see the Lord's fingerprints wherever you go. There are documented stories of miraculous healings, not just physical healings but ecological healings—barren trees now producing fruit, stagnant lagoons teeming with fish, poisonous waters now fresh and clean. Many political leaders and tribal chiefs profess Jesus as Lord. Even villages that once practiced cannibalism now lift up the name of Jesus.

In 2006, I visited Suva to speak at the Sentinel Group's Global Summit. While there, Suliasi invited me to preach at his church that Sunday morning, so I moved to a hotel in the city of Nadi (pronounced "Nandee") to be closer to the airport. From my hotel room, I could literally walk out the back door and be on the beach, but instead I worked inside.

There were floods back home in Houston, and a fire had just destroyed the warehouse of one of our ministry partners. I was wondering if I should cut my trip short and go home early. In addition to that, I was having problems with my computer. Suddenly, out of nowhere, the ceiling in my room caved in and water came pouring down! I found out later that a worker on the second floor had busted a water pipe. Now it wasn't just flooding in Houston, it was also flooding in my room in Fiji! I quickly grabbed my belongings off the floor so they wouldn't be ruined, and I called the front desk.

As the bellman helped me move to another room, he sensed my frustration. "Pastor Stringer," he said, "can I pray for you?" I was a little surprised that he knew who I was. He must have sensed that, for he continued, "Yes, we all know you. When you preach at Pastor Suliasi's church, we see you on television, and many of us have read your books." He told me that there were twenty believers working at the hotel, pastors and intercessors whose ministry was to pray for and serve the guests who stay there. In their own quiet way, they are still influencing the nations right where they are.

This is not a unique situation. Throughout Fiji, there are so many people with spirits so gentle and humble who truly love Jesus, who quietly yet proudly declare Christ as Lord. As they go about their work, they hum praise songs to Jesus.

Does this mean that the country is completely free of all problems? No—not by any means—but God is definitely at work in their midst. He has honored the prayers of a handful of men and women who, years ago, cried out, "Lord, give us our nation!" And now, the Father of all nations and all generations is taking them to other nations of the world with this same message.

EVERY NATION, EVERY ETHNICITY

When we say God will give us the nations, does this mean every single nation will one day be a Christian nation? We can answer only by looking at Scripture. One of the Greek words for *nation* is "ethnos," as we see in Luke 21:10. From this term, we get our words *ethnic* and *ethnicity*. I believe Scripture is revealing that, one day, people from every nationality and every ethnicity will come to the revelation knowledge of Jesus as Lord.

I experienced a glimpse of this in September 2000 when founder of the All Nations Convocation, Tom Hess, hosted 1,500 delegates in Jerusalem. From the top tower of our hotel, we could look down one side and see Bethlehem and down the other side and see the Old City of Jerusalem. It was a great vantage point for prayer, and all the intercessors took turns going up there to pray. We had with us Jewish, Arab, Persian, Japanese, Chinese, Korean, African, Hispanic, Latino believers—people from nearly every ethnicity who had come together to pray. It was a beautiful depiction of Micah 4, as we exchanged our weapons of warfare for harvesting tools.

I believe Scripture is revealing that, one day, people from every nationality and every ethnicity will come to the revelation knowledge of Jesus as Lord.

While we were there, the intifada, a Palestinian uprising against the Israeli occupancy of the West Bank and Gaza Strip, erupted. What a contrast to what was happening at the convocation! There we were, laboring in commonality in Jesus Christ, and then all this conflict broke out between the Muslims and the Jews.

News reports every morning and every night painted a graphic picture of hatred between these people groups, so why didn't the people in our group, diverse as it was, experience any hatred toward one another? What was the difference? What was the reason for the contrast? The only difference was this: Our group had a revelation of the love of Christ! We had a common bond in our relationship with Jesus.

When we come to the revelation of Jesus as the Prince of Peace, He gives us access to the Father with open arms. Then we can set aside our differences and reach a deeper level of relationship and intimacy with God and one another. Arabic, Jewish, and other Christians can worship together because of the commonality they have in relationship with Jesus Christ. No one can deny the power of God's love when witnessing the depth of relationship among opposing people groups—groups who cannot get along in the natural. When they come to the revelation of Jesus, His work on the cross, and the power of His resurrection, natural barriers are done away with.

ROOTS OF REJECTION

When the intifada began, we began thinking about the conflict in relation to the reason we were there—to worship God—and we recognized the correlation. The surface issue was one of worship: whom will we worship and who will control the site of worship? Jews, Christians, and Muslims all recognize the Temple Mount as a holy site, but their conflict goes much deeper than who will control the site. In fact, the conflict dates all the way back to Abraham and is rooted in much woundedness and bitterness.

Abraham had one son, Ishmael, with Sarah's servant Hagar; one son, Isaac, with Sarah, his wife; and six sons with Keturah, the concubine he married after Sarah's death. In Genesis 21:14, Hagar and Ishmael are sent away to live in the desert, but God promised Hagar that a great nation would come from Ishmael. (See verse 18.) His descendants are the modern-day Arabs. Abraham also sent away the sons of Keturah, and historians say that they settled in Persia (Iran) and Assyria, which includes the regions of modern-day Lebanon, Iraq, Iran, Syria, northern Jordan, and parts of western Afghanistan.

Although God blessed all Abraham's sons and provided for them, Isaac was the son of promise, the one who received Abraham's blessing and inheritance from God, according to biblical Scripture.

Isaac's son Esau was born just before his twin brother, Jacob, and married into the family of his uncle Ishmael. (See Genesis 28:9.) It's interesting that both Ishmael and Esau were firstborn sons who did not receive the family blessing reserved for them. So we see two slighted older brothers marrying into each other's lineage, resulting in a double portion of woundedness.

This raises an important question. Could it be that when an individual carries deep-rooted woundedness, he imparts it to others around him and even carries it down to generations to come? Can the result be widespread woundedness? It seems that we still contend with a group of nations—the descendants of Ishmael, Esau (also known as "Edom," whose descendants carry a deep animosity toward the Jews), and Keturah—that want to make something happen by force because they did not receive their fathers' blessing.

Muslims, Jews, and Christians all have commonality in Father Abraham, who is a type of the heavenly father, yet they are in conflict with one another! Regardless of our political or even religious opinions of what is going on in the world, we cannot deny that there are generations of brothers, sons, and cousins fighting among themselves. What began as a root of bitterness in few individuals has been carried down from generation to generation, affecting entire nations.

This is why it is so important for us to submit our hurts to the Father for healing and to practice forgiveness. When we operate out of wounds and bitterness, we hinder our intimacy with others as well as our intimacy with God.

See to it that no one falls short of the grace of God and that no bitter root grows up to cause trouble and defile many.

(Hebrews 12:15 NIV)

Furthermore, as Colossians 1:12 tells us, we are to give *"thanks to the Father who has qualified us to be partakers of the inheritance of the saints in the light."*

No matter who we are or where we are from, God Himself qualifies us to receive His inheritance! He is the Father who embraces us all through the love He displayed through Christ and the work of the cross.

AN INHERITANCE FOR ALL

Desiring blessings is not limited to any single nation or religion. Everyone is looking for identity. Everyone wants a connection with the Creator. Everyone wants the love of a father. But it will not happen unless we put Jesus on the throne, for to know the Father, we must first know the Son. (See Matthew 11:27.) Then we can exchange our wounded spirits for His Spirit of adoption.

I don't want to bring wounds from my past into my present relationships, and Scripture tells me I am empowered to pull down every vain imagination. (See 2 Corinthians 10:5.) A love of truth helps me to positively respond instead of negatively react to old insecurities, hurts, and pains.

We can continue to react to old wounds, which may have been passed down through the generations, or we can let the Son direct us to the open arms of the heavenly Father, in which we are set free, healed, affirmed, approved, and accepted.

God wants all nations and all generations to know that He has an inheritance for them. He wants to adopt us and heal our lands, but we need His presence. That's what we've seen so beautifully in nations like Fiji, where people of different backgrounds have been able to reconcile through their commonality in Christ, in spite of all tension and conflict going on around them.

God wants all nations and all generations to know that He has an inheritance for them. He wants to adopt us and heal our lands, but we need His presence.

When we realize who Jesus is and surrender to the sealing of the Spirit of adoption, God changes our hearts and enables us to touch the nations. The heavenly Father wants to reveal Himself to and pour out His blessings on the wandering generations and orphaned nations.

He offers us an inheritance through His Son, Jesus, and that inheritance is the nations of the world! From urban mission groups to unreached people groups, from inner cities to foreign mission fields, from wherever we are now to the uttermost parts of the earth, God wants to give us the nations because He is the Father of all nations! And as we become His children through the Spirit of adoption, the nations will become our inheritance, as well!

The church is God's tool and His answer to the despair in the nations of the world today. As never before, we see fatherless nations, spiritual orphans, in search of identity. We see both human and natural disasters. We see generations in the deserts of life, scattered, looking for a place to belong and a land to possess. We must show the nations and the generations that God has already given us an awesome work of grace that entitles us to His whole inheritance! We don't have to strive for it. We don't have to fight for it. We don't have to take it by force, according to the flesh. We take it by promise through God's Son, Jesus!

The raging battles of our time must be fought on our knees, for we wrestle not with flesh and blood. (See Ephesians 6:12.) I love to quote Francis of Assisi, who said, "Preach the gospel at all times. If necessary, use words." Let us make ourselves available to carry this message of good news to the nations, that they may know the richness of the blessings that await them through the Father of all nations and all generations!

12

THE SPIRIT
OF ADOPTION

As a boy, I remember wanting to be with my father so badly and so often; but he wasn't there, so I would sit outside my house in the fort I built, just me and my little dog, Bambi.

Dad was in the military, so that often took him away. He struggled with alcohol, so even when he was around, he wasn't really there. After he and my mother divorced, he was gone until I met him again in 1978, when I moved to Houston to find him. My family was living in Washington state at the time, but I was restless, always trying to fill the void of my father's absence. I knew that something was missing in my life. I felt as if things would fall into place if I could just find my dad, so I contacted the military to find out where he was. He was living in Houston, and they agreed to let him know I was looking for him. Like this emerging generation in pursuit of spiritual fathers, I was in pursuit of my earthly father. It was a journey that ultimately led me to my heavenly Father.

My dad had remarried when I found him, and he had a daughter, Judy. I was happy to see that his life had changed. But even so, it was hard for us to connect because of all the years that had passed. We really loved each other, but neither of us knew how to express it or how to recover the intimacy that had been lost over the many years of disconnection.

In 1990, I began to have a better understanding of my dad's life when I accompanied seventeen veterans on a trip back to Vietnam for healing. For fifteen years, these Christian men had struggled with nightmares, drugs, and alcohol. They had problems in their marriages. They suffered "survivor's guilt," having watched their friends die right before their eyes.

As we approached our destination and the plane began its descent, you could have heard a pin drop. I watched these men as they looked out the windows of the plane, tears streaming down their faces. Over the next few days, as I listened to them, observed them, and saw the pain in their lives, I began to understand why my own father and stepfather—who both had served in Vietnam—didn't know how to engage with me as their son and why they, too, had turned to alcohol to cover up the memories and the atrocities of the war. It made me love them even more and gave me the heart of God to see them saved, healed, and delivered.

In 1993, I was away on a ministry trip when I got word that my dad had been diagnosed with military-related lung cancer. At that time, Dad had not been drinking or smoking for ten years. His wife, Margaret, had noticed he was reading his Bible in the mornings. Once when I was traveling, I asked a pastor friend to visit him for me. Afterward, my friend told me my dad had been listening to the Bible on tape for over a year. He had read my books and was listening to my teaching tapes. The pastor assured me that my dad had a relationship with Jesus.

My dad began to reach out to me, trying to reconnect. He wanted to talk to his son, Doug. He would say things like, "Remember the time we did this?" and "Remember the time we did that?" I realized that there were so many memories I had stuffed because all I could recall were the times he wasn't there. He wanted to bring back the past we had lost, but I didn't know how to receive from him or how to reach out to him.

The entire time he was sick, my dad never complained. As his illness progressed, I would call him to see how he was doing, and his answer was always the same: "I'm fine; things are great!"

I always promised him I would go see him whenever I got back from my next trip, but it never happened. Margaret started calling me to say,

"Doug, you really need to go see him. He's not doing well." For a whole week, I planned to see him, but things kept coming up. It was finally Friday, and I was doing a two-hour program at a local radio station. I had every intention of seeing him as soon as I finished, but in the middle of the show, I got a "911" message on my beeper from Cynthia at the office trying to reach me: "Doug, I don't know how to tell you this," she said when I called, "but your dad has passed away."

All week, the Holy Spirit had been nudging me, saying, *"Go see your father; go see your father"*; but I was too busy doing "God's" work. The doctors had told us he had six months to live, but it was only ninety days later and he was gone. I remember sitting on the couch in that radio station trying to deal with all my emotions. I didn't know what to say or what to do. The song "Cats in the Cradle" by Harry Chapin kept playing over and over in my head. The song speaks first of a little boy who wanted to be with his dad, but his dad never had time for him. When the dad grew older, the tables were turned. Now the dad wanted to be with his son, but the son had his own life, and there was no time for Dad. At that moment, I realized how that had happened in my own life, and how much I regretted the past week of missed opportunities.

We live lives full of missed opportunities. How many times do we put aside those we love because we're too busy for them? We're too busy to tell our parents, our children, our husbands, and our wives "I love you." How many times do we walk out the door frustrated with the ones we love? Yet we have no certainty we will see that person again; we have no guarantees about tomorrow. We must cherish what we have and take advantage of the moments with the people God has placed in our lives.

We must cherish what we have and take advantage of the moments with the people God has placed in our lives.

Likewise, how many times do we neglect our heavenly Father, our Abba, who wants so much to seal us with His Spirit of adoption, to make us children in His family? How often do we forget that He wants to give us a new name in life, a new position in life? He is the One who has gone to such great lengths to bring us into His family, yet how often do we still neglect Him?

> *For God so loved the world that He gave His only begotten Son, that whoever believes in Him should not perish but have everlasting life.*   (John 3:16)

We go about our lives wanting Him to be our "sugar daddy" instead of our Abba-Father, the One whose lap we can crawl into as we tell Him our struggles and the difficulties we're going through: "Oh, Father! I need Your wisdom. I need Your love. I need Your direction. I'm lonely today. I'm hurting today. Would you just hold on to me and speak to me?"

He wants that from us so much! He wanted it so much that He gave His only begotten Son so we could be sealed with the Spirit of adoption and made sons and daughters in His family. Let's not miss out on opportunities to draw close to our friends and our families, but let's especially not neglect so great a salvation, so great a love from our Father!

God desires His best for us: a revelation of the Father, the identity of the Father, the embrace of the Father. That really is what the Spirit of adoption is all about. And it comes with a promise—joint heirship with His Son, Jesus Christ, because in Him, we, too, are children of God.

Yes, I was a boy who so badly wanted a father, but my heavenly Father was there for me; He is there for all of us. And now He can help us be good fathers and mothers to a generation pursuing spiritual fathers and mothers. We don't know how to do it, but He can give us the grace. He can teach us how to parent this emerging, orphaned, fatherless generation that needs direction. He can teach us how to be their covering and how to introduce them to their heavenly Father.

A NEW NAME

When influential pastor Jack Hayford's mother went to be with the Lord, he spoke of the inheritance he and his brother Jim received after her homegoing. "It wasn't that we were worthy in ourselves to receive the inheritance but only because we carried the name 'Hayford.' We automatically received an inheritance because of the name."

Because we've been purchased by the blood of Jesus, we now have a new God-given name and an inheritance. This is not because of our good works or because we've earned it but because we are sealed by His name. Scripture says,

> *In Him you also trusted, after you heard the word of truth, the gospel of your salvation; in whom also, having believed, you were sealed with the Holy Spirit of promise.*   (Ephesians 1:13)

The Spirit of adoption is really the Spirit of promise—the promise of a new life. If we are His children, then we are *"heirs—heirs of God and joint heirs with Christ, if indeed we suffer with Him, that we may also be glorified together"* (Romans 8:17). The root of the Hebrew word used here for *"suffer"* (*sumpascho*) is the word for "passion" (*pascho*). If we have fellowship in Christ's sufferings, then we have the passion of Christ in us and a heart to do His will.

Because we are heirs with Jesus, we are qualified to assume God the Father's divine power and nature.

> *Even to them I will give in My house and within My walls a place and a name better than that of sons and daughters; I will give them an everlasting name that shall not be cut off.*   (Isaiah 56:5)

The old ways of sin and death are overtaken with Christ's life, which moves us into a position of adoption, a place of promise. He gives us a new life, a new name, and a new status in life, then seals us with the Spirit.

GENUINE SONS

The term "adoption" implies the act of officially taking the child of another to be one's own. The finished work of the cross, through grace, is how we become God's adopted children, and the Spirit certifies this sonship.

For as many as are led by the Spirit of God, these are the sons of God. For you did not receive the spirit of bondage again to fear, but you received the Spirit of adoption by whom we cry out, "Abba, Father."   (Romans 8:14–15)

The Aramaic here is "Abba," which we already know can be translated "Daddy," or "Papa." Imagine crawling into your father's lap and saying, "Hey, Papa," or "Hey, Daddy," or "Hey, Abba."

God is bringing us into this place of adoption by which we can call Him "Abba." It's no longer God out in the cosmic universe and you and me down here as grains of sand on the earth. He knows us by name. He knew us when we were in our mothers' wombs. He wants to have an intimate relationship with us. He wants us to call Him "Abba."

God is bringing us into this place of adoption by which we can call Him "Abba." It's no longer God out in the cosmic universe and you and me down here as grains of sand on the earth. He knows us by name.

Jesus used that same term in the garden of Gethsemane, when He cried, "Abba!" (See Mark 14:36.) Likewise, in each and every one of our lives—no matter what struggles, fears, or insecurities we encounter—we can come boldly before the Lord, as a child comes to his papa, when the Spirit of adoption has sealed, verified, and certified that we are truly children of the living God.

Literally translated, the Greek word for "adoption" means "placing as a son."[27] It means that we are now genuine sons—we are part of the bloodline! We have been made sons and daughters in the family of God. We are not adopted just on paper, but we carry His name.

But seek first the kingdom of God and His righteousness, and all these things shall be added to you.   (Matthew 6:33)

---

27. *huiothesia, Strong's Concordance,* http://biblehub.com/greek/5206.htm.

We have not only the promise of inheritance but also all the benefits of being in God's family. Not only are our new names written in the Lamb's Book of Life, but we are also given the promise of inheritance and the benefits of the kingdom. It's a legal placement into the family of God, a new positioning, a new identity with a promise! Let us give thanks to God for our inheritance.

RESTORING BROKEN TRUST

My mom, dad, and stepdad all are with Jesus now, and I praise the Lord that they all came to salvation before their homegoings. But growing up was difficult. I was nine when my father and mother divorced. My mother remarried, and my stepfather was an atheist. We got along really well when he wasn't drinking. But because of the alcohol, I never knew how he was going to react in any given situation. I was already dealing with my own hurts from the separation from my father, so I put up walls and sometimes reacted in rebellion.

What I didn't understand was that my father and stepfather both had hurts and issues of their own, which I could not see until I had grown. My dad had lost a teenage daughter from his first marriage in a car accident on her first date. My stepfather had no relationship with his biological father, who had been in prison, although his stepfather loved him as a son. They both had issues from serving in the Vietnam War, and my dad had also served in the Korean War.

As a child, however, I could not understand all these things. This is not meant to excuse or justify their abusive or alcoholic acts, but sometimes even as Christian adults, we find it easy to criticize authority figures—our parents, our spiritual coverings, and our pastors. We have such high expectations of them. We don't see that they, too, have deep soul wounds. Just like us, they have issues to work through, and that can happen only through a connection with the heavenly Father.

If we have had bad experiences with our fathers, we often have trouble receiving God as our Father. We have difficulty trusting Him. We must break away from the fears of earthly situations and understand that we can trust God. He knows exactly what our needs are, and He will never leave us or forsake us. (See Deuteronomy 31:6.)

"I'LL BE YOUR FATHER"

When I became a Christian, Dr. Cole became a spiritual father to me. In 1989, he invited me to attend a men's event with him. It was a large father-son gathering at a church in Dallas.

Dr. Cole called me and said, "Doug, I just want to make sure you're coming to Dallas for the men's event."

"No, sir, I won't be coming," I said. I was going through some difficult situations, and I just didn't feel like being around people.

But Dr. Cole persisted. "Doug, you really need to be there."

Finally, I relented, and I honored Dr. Cole by going to the event. As I boarded the plane, I hadn't eaten in over two weeks—not by choice but because I had felt compelled by the Spirit to fast. I was grieving in my heart about a lot of things, and now I was on my way to this event for fathers and sons, when I never even felt like I had a father. As a Christian, I had come to know Jesus but not the Father's heart and the Father's love. I understood the cross, I understood grace, but I still didn't understand the Spirit of adoption or have intimacy with the Father. Because of my upbringing, it was difficult to understand God as Abba.

During the event, Dr. Cole gave an invitation to come to the altar. Hundreds of men were there—fathers and their sons—and I watched them running to the altar, embracing, repenting, and forgiving. Tears of joy began to stream down my face for that emerging generation and their fathers, but mingled with them were tears of sadness and a longing for the love and companionship of a father. Occasionally, I had done special things with my father and stepfather, but it was never consistent. I had never learned to ski. I had never learned to swim. I had never been deep-sea fishing. Here I was, already in my thirties, and there was a whole list of things I had never done, normal things that were done between sons and fathers.

"Doug," I heard God say in a still, small voice, "I'm your Father. I want to do things with you that you never did with a father."

My response was somewhat skeptical. I couldn't comprehend how I could have that kind of companionship with Someone who wasn't human, who wasn't tangible. Besides, how could I, as an adult, go back to being a son?

A year later, I was on the ski slopes of Crested Butte, Colorado. I took the "Never Ever" class and watched seven-year-olds with no poles zip past me. I thought skiing was the stupidest sport I had ever taken part in. But, finally, after a couple of days, I was actually skiing one of the slopes. And though I was still falling a lot, it didn't matter anymore.

At one point, I stopped and looked at the beauty of God's creation. Suddenly, the Lord spoke to me, reminding me of His promise and all the things we had done together throughout that year. I had gone deep-sea fishing for the first time in my life with pastor friends in Australia, and I caught the biggest fish of the entire group—it was huge! I called it "Jaws." None of the other pastors had caught anything that size the entire summer. I had played golf for the first time in Australia, too, and I hit the same kangaroo twice! Now my staff jokes that every time I go to Australia, the kangaroos put on their crash helmets. During that same year, I went to a lake, jumped off a boat, and went water skiing for the first time. I never did get up, so it was more like "knee boarding," but I did it! Me and my Father, me and my Abba. And recently, I was snow skiing in the Rocky Mountains!

As I looked back on that year and all the things I did for the first time, I realized that my heavenly Father had become my Abba-Father. He had kept His promise and had become tangible to me through the Spirit of adoption.

LEARNING TO BE SONS

Even as a Christian, it took me years to realize that my Father in heaven had an inheritance for me. I could believe that for everyone else. I could pray and agree and see God do miracles for others, but not for

The Spirit of Adoption   141

me. After all, an inheritance is passed from father to son, and I didn't even know how to be a son.

When we look in Scripture, we can see examples of good sons and bad sons, both in the spiritual and in the natural. Elisha was a son to Elijah, and he received a double portion of his father's anointing because he honored him. Gehazi, Elisha's servant, could have been a son, too, but instead chose to dishonor Elisha by going behind his back and asking Naaman for a reward. (See 2 Kings 5:20–27.) He was stricken with leprosy because of his unfaithfulness.

Elisha was persistent and stayed with Elijah, not because he wanted an inheritance of monetary value or even because he wanted a double portion of Elijah's anointing; he sought after the prophet because he wanted to be with him as he lived his everyday life in God. He knew that being in the presence of the prophet was priceless. He stayed with his mentor until his death because he dearly loved him, not because of some future benefit he'd receive only after witnessing Elijah's death.

Earlier, I shared some thoughts of Pastor Mike concerning the marks of a father. A son, he says, is someone who stays, who doesn't leave just because he is corrected. A son does not operate in the flesh; he is led by the Spirit. (See Romans 8:14.) He cares about his father's work and ministry, unlike Hophni and Phineas, who destroyed the ministry of their father, Eli the priest.

I was invited to sit in on a roundtable of leaders of the emerging generations, hosted by Mission America in New York City. "To have spiritual fathers in the room brought everything up to a greater level," said one of our hosts. "Their presence and spoken words of exhortation challenged the group and kept things connected through another perspective."

A son recognizes the value of just being in his father's presence.

HE WAS THERE ALL ALONG

I used to lament the fact that I had missed out on so many father-son opportunities with my earthly father and stepfather. But after God adopted me, I realized that my heavenly Father was with me all along.

God wants to be a Father to the fatherless, to adopt them in these fatherless days. He wants to nurture and care for us, to give us His nature and power, yet He also chastises and disciplines us. Some of you may experience lives of chaos because you never had a father to discipline you. But God desires to discipline you, and in His discipline, there is peace. God's discipline is a good thing. (See Proverbs 3:12; Hebrews 12:6.)

Quite simply, God wants to adopt us, to take ownership of us, to make us His children. He wants to give us His inheritance, His love, even His discipline. He wants us to take on His name, His legacy, and His lineage. He wants to take care of and nurture us in ways far greater than any earthly father ever could. He desperately wants to be a Father to the fatherless, to seal us into His family by the Spirit of adoption.

13

"DOUGIE, FIX IT?"

The burdens of the world are too much to bear alone, but with the empowerment of the Holy Spirit, we can present Him to others. If we give people hope and direct them to the Father, with His Spirit, He'll take care of the rest. We must return to the Scriptures and look to the God of all generations and all nations, who seals us with the Spirit of adoption through Jesus Christ, for direction.

I met with a pastor and his wife from Brazil who were visiting Houston and praying about planting a church here. They told me about their ministry to street kids in Rio de Janeiro and how they once asked a seven-year-old boy who his father was. The child answered with what they believed to be the name of a demonic spirit.

What a tragedy! Because these children don't know who their fathers are, they adopt the names of demons. However, because this couple and their co-laborers' tangible expression of Christ to this little orphan boy, he now answers that same question with "Jesus." He has become part of the emerging prophetic generation, adopted into the family of the heavenly Father through faith in the Son.

Just as John the Baptist was anointed and empowered to usher in the arrival of Christ, so the emerging generation is anointed to usher in a great outpouring of God's presence in preparation for Christ's return. And just as God wants to adopt them, so, too, the enemy desires to be their counterfeit father.

Just as John the Baptist was anointed and empowered to usher in the arrival of Christ, so the emerging generation is anointed to usher in a great outpouring of God's presence in preparation for Christ's return.

Sam, a marketplace minister in Hollywood, says, "Every battle in history with the saints of God has been a battle through which Satan challenged God's authority." In effect, Satan does so by asking the question, "Who's your daddy?" If he can successfully remove our children's biological fathers, he stands a better chance of usurping God's role of Father, as well. We must not be negligent in exposing him as a counterfeit!

"DOUGIE, FIX IT!"

My sister Jeanne, and brother, Kenny, are nine and ten years younger than me. Growing up, I helped take care of them, so I became a father figure to them.

When we were young, Jeanne slipped away from the house one day while I was at school. The police found her blocks away and were driving her up and down the streets to help her find her house when my mom spotted her in the police car. "Mommy! Mommy!" Jeanne cried when she saw her.

It turns out that Jeanne had been looking for her big brother Dougie, so she'd sneaked out the front gate and headed for the Little League field where she watched me play ball. The field was a couple of miles from the house and across a busy highway!

When she was older, she put all my sports trophies in a pillowcase and slept with them. One time, she took them with her to school for show-and-tell.

I took Jeanne and Kenny everywhere I went. They looked up to me and wanted to be with me all the time. When they were scared, they slept in my room, and whenever something went wrong, they would often bring the problem to me, hoping I could fix it.

In 1994, we found out that my stepfather (their biological father) had just been diagnosed with military-related lung cancer—just as my dad had been diagnosed one year earlier—and we drove from Houston to Waco to see him. By then, my little sister was not only a grown adult but also a wife and mom. I'll never forget how she looked at me that day in the car—distraught at the thought of losing her father to cancer—and said, "Dougie, fix it."

At that moment, I was seized with an overwhelming sense of responsibility and the ache of not knowing what to do. I had been so used by the Lord all over the world, and here I was now, wanting so much to be there for my little brother and sister, yet feeling so helpless. This time, Dougie couldn't fix it.

But our heavenly Father can fix any situation, though it's not always the way we want Him to do it. My stepdad passed away six months later, but when he left us, he went to be with Jesus.

Years before, I had shared the gospel with him and had given him a Bible. He had professed to know Christ at one time, and I had led him in a salvation prayer. But though he had no longer been an atheist, and I'd rejoiced in that, he'd still had struggles and challenges in his newfound journey. His illness, however, brought him to a place of really considering all that the Lord had spoken to him in the previous few years. During those six months, we were assured that he had totally given his life to Jesus, and so we are secure in knowing he is rejoicing in heaven.

In addition to Jeanne and Kenny, I have a half sister, Judy, who was born to my dad after he remarried after the divorce. When I met Judy, I was already grown and she was in elementary school. Judy didn't want to take my trophies to show-and-tell—she wanted to take me! It was such a novel thing for her to learn she had an older Japanese brother.

Years after our father passed away, Judy called and left a message on my voice mail at work. One time, our ministry had partnered with

Christian Broadcasting Network to distribute 500,000 copies of *The Book of Hope* throughout the city. She had come across one of these copies and saw our Somebody Cares stamp on the inside cover. She had been praying to Jesus but still had not been able to come to grips with the loss of our father. She was his little girl, and she adored him. "I just don't understand why Dad had to die," she said tearfully in her message.

She could not understand why God didn't fix it. But in reality, He did! Dad had given his life to Christ, and he is now with Jesus in heaven. And even though I go through moments of missing my biological father, my stepfather, and my mother, there remains a supernatural peace that surpasses all understanding in knowing that they all are dancing with Jesus! I know we will meet again and rejoice together for eternity at the throne of the Lord because we all have the same Daddy!

A GOD OF REDEMPTION

I praise God for His redemptive power and how He allowed me to see it in my dad's life. He allowed me to see my father free from alcohol and to be a part of his salvation experience as he read my books and listened to my teaching tapes. Furthermore, there was such beauty in the way he loved and spoiled Judy; she really was Daddy's little girl.

Years later, his wife Margaret said to me, "If you only knew how proud he was to have you as a son. He just didn't know how to tell you." Many of us have difficulty expressing ourselves to our spouses, children, and other loved ones, which is a hindrance to our ability to connect with one another. We are not able to express our affirmation, approval, and acceptance. That's why I say now, "Communication is a key to life."

When my stepdad was diagnosed with cancer, I was determined not to miss the last days of his life as I did with my father. Often I commuted to Waco during that time to be with him.

That six months was a beautiful time of reminiscing and reflection, laughter, and tears. He often told us he loved us and asked us to take care of our mom. We realized that even though we'd experienced a lot of dysfunction, we still had been a family the best we knew how. He really had been a father to me because he'd been there for me; at least, he'd come to my games. Even if he didn't know how to express it, I knew he loved me and was proud to consider me a son.

I saw God's redemption once again as my stepfather poured his life and love into Jeanne's and Kenny's children in his later years. Even though he had not known how to be a good father to us when we were growing up, he was a very good grandfather. He would take my mom and the kids camping and fishing and on other outings. He spent so much time with them.

Our God is a God of redemption and reconciliation. It is important to give our parents the grace to change when God begins to move in their lives. Just as we desire for others not to hold us to our pasts, we must not hold others to their pasts, but acknowledge who they have become or who they *can become* in Christ. This is one of the ways we honor God by honoring our parents. And just as Shem and Japheth did for their father, Noah, we can choose to cover their nakedness. (See Genesis 9:23.)

THE PRAYERS OF A CHILD

And [Jesus] said to them, "Why did you seek Me? Did you not know that I must be about My Father's business?" (Luke 2:49)

At the young age of twelve, Jesus knew who His Father was. We, too, must have that same kind of faith or we will never enter into the fullness of the kingdom.

Assuredly, I say to you, whoever does not receive the kingdom of God as a little child will by no means enter it.
(Mark 10:15, Luke 18:17)

Before Jeanne was born, I had asked God for a little sister. "I promise I'll teach her all about You," I had said to Him. A year later, my mother had been expecting another baby. Then I prayed again, "God, You gave me a sister, and I am so thankful. Now, if you give me a brother, I'll teach him about You, too." He answered my prayer again; Kenny was born, but this time, there were complications.

Kenny came four months early. He had pneumonia and a hernia and had to have two eye operations. It was questionable if he would even live. Doctors said that if he did live, he would be "slow" or maybe even a "vegetable." I sat in the car outside the hospital and cried to the Lord on behalf of my little brother. "Jesus, please! You gave me a sister a year ago; now You gave me a brother. The doctors say he might not live, but I don't believe that. Please make him healthy!"

Once again, God heard the petitions of a little boy who didn't even know that much about Him. Kenny not only survived but overcame all those challenges, barriers, and obstacles; he become a sharp, intelligent young man. He went to a technical institute, then joined the Navy to follow in the footsteps of his father. Later, he moved to Houston and worked in banking.

Kenny went through a difficult and painful divorce that left some deep emotional wounds and compounded other challenges and issues he is going through today. His children now live out of state, and because he desired to see them more often, he left his job in banking to become a flight attendant. He called me after one of his trips just to leave a message that he had gotten to spend time with them on one four-day layover near their home.

A few weeks prior to that, he had called after returning from one of his first trips with the airline.

"What are you doing?" he'd asked.

"I'm having dinner with friends. Are you hungry?"

"No, I already ate. I just wanted to talk to you."

"We'll wait for you," I'd said. "Come on over."

I'd hung up the phone and said to my friends, "He wants me to see him in his flight attendant's uniform."

Sure enough, Kenny had come straight from the airport so big brother Doug could see him in his uniform! Even now, he still looks to me as a father figure who gives him affirmation, acceptance, and approval.

In their early years, I taught Jeanne and Kenny about God, but in my teenage years, I departed from His ways and was not faithful to the promise I'd made to Him so many years earlier. For a season, I left home and was estranged from my family. That's when Jeanne began sleeping with my sports trophies. The day she took them with her to school for show-and-tell, I told her to wait for me after school and I would meet her there. She sat on the curb for hours, but I never showed up. There were so many times I failed them.

Yet God was faithful in spite of it all, and He watched out for them. My prayer for Kenny, Jeanne, and Judy continues to be that they would grow in relationship with their heavenly Father, who loves them in a way no parent or big brother ever could. He will never leave them or forsake them. He will never fail them.

WHO'S YOUR DADDY NOW?

When Jesus taught the disciples to pray using the endearment "Father," He knew the power of coming to God and knowing Him as Father and us as His children.

Likewise, when those around us ask, "Who's your daddy?" we must know in our heart of hearts that the divine Creator is also a Father who loves us, accepts us, liberates us, and empowers us, no matter who we are or where we're from.

Are you from the former generation who did not understand how to parent because they did not have proper role models in their own lives?

Are you from the emerging generation who are looking for spiritual fathers to bless them, release them into their destinies, and give them approval, affirmation, and acceptance?

Are you one of those "camels" wandering in the wilderness, who have never come to a knowledge of Jesus as Savior?

No matter who you are, the Father waits for you with open arms. All the riches of God await you in His presence. He has an inheritance for you, He has a destiny for you, and He wants to bring you into His family through the Spirit of adoption. All you need to do is receive Him by faith in His Son. (See Romans 10:9; Acts 16:31; John 3:16.)

All the riches of God await you in His presence. He has an inheritance for you, He has a destiny for you, and He wants to bring you into His family through the Spirit of adoption.

One night, I was in New England preparing to preach the next day. When I checked my voice mail before going to bed, I had a message from Jeanne. One of her friends had just miscarried. As she was grieving for her friend's loss, she began reflecting on her own family and the many ways God had blessed her. She called me just to let me know she was thinking about me.

"I don't know if you can understand the impact you've had on my life. The earliest memories I have are of you taking care of me and protecting me," she said. "Other people know you as 'Pastor Doug,' but I know you as 'Dougie.' I am so blessed to have two wonderful brothers who love me. No one loves you as I do. You introduced me to my Father in heaven, and I am so thankful for that."

Because I was a father figure to my little brother and sister, I can now remind them who their Daddy is. There is a God in heaven, and He loves them. He rocks! He can fix it! All they need to know is that they can turn to Him and He will be there for them.

I say the same thing to each of you. Are you willing to receive God as your Father through the spirit of adoption?

In light of all fatherless generations, we must ask ourselves, "Who's my daddy?"

Have our past choices brought hurt or disappointment to others? Certainly, we have experienced pain and dysfunction. We cannot change our pasts, but the choices we make today will affect our futures. We can choose now to look upon our heavenly Father, who can be tangible to us. We can call Him "Abba." He is the One who will never disappoint us, who will never forsake us. And we know Him through His Son, Jesus, because to know the Son is to know the Father. (See Matthew 11:27; Luke 10:22.)

Let Him embrace you with His tangible presence. Know that you are fully accepted, affirmed, and approved, and you have an inheritance waiting for you. Receive the Father's blessing.

Who's your Daddy now?

ADDENDUM

God has a heart that is specifically attuned to the needs of those on the fringes—the lost, lonely, and forgotten. We see it in Jesus' ministry when He took time for the woman at the well and when he allowed a woman with a scandalous past to wash His feet. Something about their desperate need and honest sincerity stirs God's heart to action. Never doubt the prayer power of a fatherless generation.

In September 2015, I was invited to speak at a fundraising banquet in preparation for United Cry DC 2016, a national call to pray at the Lincoln Memorial for thousands of pastors and denominational leaders. After speaking, I was asked if I was aware that a young man, Derek Sewell, had just completed a forty-day fast on my behalf. He had heard that only a few months prior, I had been diagnosed with 80% aggressive B-Cell Lymphoma and he felt compelled to intercede for me.

I had first met Derek and other young leaders a couple years before. I could sense the authenticity and hunger for revival in their generation. Whenever I spoke at functions in the Dallas/Fort Worth area, they tried to connect with me over a meal or coffee. I was deeply moved by Derek's heart-felt sacrifice and support. When I asked Derek why he felt compelled to go to such lengths for me he shared that he had lost his father to cancer when he was a teenager and that he was fasting and praying for me in obedience to a dream the Lord had given him. He said, "In the dream, I heard the voice of the Lord say, 'Doug Stringer is a father in this nation and a father in this generation. As you intercede and pray for his healing, you will be interceding for America as well.'" When he awoke, he knew that his commitment to fast and pray for me was because I was serving as a spiritual father to his generation. He had already lost his earthly father to cancer and now he knew he was battling for this generation of spiritual fathers. He also shared with me that in his dream I was healed. He had only told his fiancée and a couple of other people about his dream and his call.

Amazingly, he completed his fast at the very time I received a good report from my doctors. You see, I was diagnosed with stage-4 cancer in the beginning of April 2015, but by mid-August, my midway P.E.T. scan and tests showed no evidence of disease. Although I continued treatments through November 2015, my doctors had given me the very good news that I was in total remission.

Needless to say, we were overwhelmed and humbled that this young man, Derek, and so many other young people around the globe had been praying, fasting, and interceding on my behalf. It was with wet eyes that we thanked Derek for such a sacrifice. I also remember getting a video from an orphanage in India with all the children there praying for me. It's a powerful thing when the GenEdge and Emerging Generation are contending for this generation of spiritual fathers and mothers.

"I WANT YOU TO BE MY DADDY!"

"Ashley, what are three things a six-year-old girl wants for her seventh birthday?" I asked her while gathered with a group at a restaurant after an evening Bible study. Emphatically, she simply replied, "I only want one thing for my birthday: I want a daddy for my birthday."

Needless to say, we were all moved by Ashley's comments. In fact, later I discovered that she and some of her friends at school and church had been praying for daddies for one another. Be it girls or boys, each of us has a longing for the presence and security of a father in the home. Most of us desire the affirmation and blessing of a father. This has been the cry of generations.

To break the silence that ensued, I asked Ashley another question: "Well, what kind of daddy do you want?" She sheepishly looked around the table, then looked at her mother, and said, "I know Mommy says that I'm not allowed to pray like this, but I know Jesus hears the prayers of children and I'm a child, so I want you to be my daddy." Obviously we were all stunned by such innocent forthrightness from such a precious little girl.

Lisa, Ashley's mother, was a bit embarrassed and reiterated that she discouraged those types of prayers. At one time, Lisa had been the first female vice president and program director for a top-40 radio station in a primary market in Southern California. After many years in the radio and music business, she found herself going through deep personal heartbreak, becoming a single mother, and having to make the tough decision to leave California and move back to the city of her birth and upbringing. During this time, her relationship with the Lord greatly deepened. Eventually, with a two-year-old daughter and widowed mother, she moved back to Texas to be near other family members. Before long, they became involved in a church, where Lisa volunteered her time by giving back to young people through a youth ministry. Later she became part of the church staff. This is where we first met and became friends.

I ministered and spoke at the church often. The pastor and other staff members and I had been friends for years. In fact, Gene, one of the elders of the church who had become like a father to Lisa, was the one who encouraged Lisa and me to meet. Reluctantly, because both of us were not interested in any sort of blind date or meeting, we did have lunch with Gene and his wife, Edell, to get acquainted as friends. It was two years of friendship building and processing, culminating in Ashley's comments in the restaurant.

Although I knew I was attracted to Lisa, I didn't exactly know if I would be a good husband and instant father. Ashley's precious heart cry, however, moved me to a place of deep prayer and reflection. I have been considered a spiritual mentor and father to many young people over the years. I've taught and written books like *The Fatherless Generation, Hope for a Fatherless Generation*, and others, yet here I was confronted by a six-year-old, who in many ways was voicing the heart cry of a generation, not looking for a perfect father, but a willing one.

I remember the evening I was invited to cook my famous Japanese ramen noodles—"famous" in my own estimation. Present were Lisa, Ashley, Lisa's mother, Gene and Edell, and Ruben and Cynthia, friends who had journeyed and chaperoned us along the way. After dinner, my heart was palpitating but I finally mustered up enough courage to ask Lisa to be wife. I remember saying that I was not only asking for her to be my wife, but for permission to make it a package deal—I wanted the blessings of Ashley and Lisa's mother too. Through everyone's tears of joy, I remember Ashley asking, "Does this mean I can start calling you Daddy tonight?" and "Can you move in tonight?" After a few minutes of joy and laughter, we explained that it would take some time for a wedding to be planned before those questions would be fulfilled.

God heard Ashley's prayers, and two days after her seventh birthday, I became her daddy! It has been more than seven years since that day and there are so many stories to tell, but we will save those for another time. One story I do want to share is one that I pray will encourage each of you.

GOD HAS NOT FORGOTTEN YOU!

When Ashley was about eight years old, I met her and Lisa for lunch. They were spending a day at Second Baptist Church, in Houston, Texas, for a Home School and Christian Curriculum convention. After lunch I mentioned I needed to go to my office for a few minutes to catch up on a few things, even though it was Saturday and my office was closed. Ashley asked if she could go with me and Mommy agreed. While we were there, Ashley was enjoying worship records that played in our ministry prayer room. I told her that I needed to leave for a few moments to go down the hall to the restroom, and that I was going to lock the doors to our offices and would be right back. Just a short time later I was walking down the hallway in the office building where our offices are, and I heard her pulling on the double glass doors, exclaiming, "Daddy, Daddy, somebody help me!"

I immediately came running down the hall and asked, "Ashley, honey, what's the matter?"

She held on to me for quite some time and finally replied, "Daddy, I thought you left me."

I assured her, "Honey, Daddy would never forget you."

She again responded, "I know you would never leave me on purpose, but I thought you forgot I was here. Besides, boys aren't supposed to take so long to go to the bathroom." We both still get a good chuckle out of that story today.

All of us, from time to time, wonder if God has forgotten us, too. I want to encourage you that your heavenly Father has not forgotten you and will not forsake you. My encouragement to each of us is that even though challenges, obstacles, and life-altering events may occur, God is still there for you with arms outstretched. His unfailing love will see you through and His plan for your life has not changed.

We receive many comments, letters, and emails pertaining to the message of this book. Here is one of the letters we received from a women's detention and correctional facility:

Hello, Mr. Stringer:

My name is V [name deleted for privacy]. Mrs. Vickie Guillory comes to minister to me every week here and she allowed me to read your book. I just have to say that some Christian books are boring (God forgive me) but I really enjoyed this one. First of all, I was raised without my father during a crucial time during my teen years, so I understand your point of view firsthand.

Until I read your book, I don't believe I've ever looked that deep into how my father's absence has affected my relationship with my heavenly Father. At this time in my life, I have a lot of time to think and I recognize many characteristics and behaviors about myself that affect my relationships. Reading your book has brought my attention to my thoughts of my relationship with God and has made me open up more and focus on why, at times, I doubt Him or why is it so hard to trust in Him like Jesus Christ did. Now when I pray to Him, I also ask Him to help me to let go and trust Him fully and to always help me to remember that He is not human that He should lie. Just to remember who He is!

I just want to say that many people don't understand that writing or speaking what's in their hearts could change a person's life drastically, as your book did for me! So I want to say thank you for doing what God put in your heart to do. You are changing people's lives! Many others are in line to read your book next! God bless you and please pray that I also follow what He puts in my heart.

Sincerely,

V

Her letter reminds us that, young and old alike, we all need to be reminded of our heavenly Father's care and embrace, regardless of our past or current circumstances.

May hope arise in you today! Call upon our heavenly Father and know that God has not forgotten you. He has a plan and a purpose for you that are far greater than any of the temporary circumstances that may be plaguing you. His Word over your life is true and He will be faithful to complete it.

I will not forget you. See, I have inscribed you on the palms of My hands. (Isaiah 49:15–16)

ABOUT THE AUTHOR

D r. Doug Stringer is founder and president of Somebody Cares America/International (SCA/SCI), which was recognized in the May/ June 2014 issue of *Ministry Today* magazine as one of the twenty-one churches or ministries that are most influencing the twenty-first-century church. Doug's years of ministry have taken him to numerous communities and nations—from urban to foreign missions, from garbage dumps to the palaces and halls of government leaders. As an Asian-American, Doug is considered a bridge-builder of reconciliation amongst various ethnic and religious groups. Doug is a sought-after international conference and crusade speaker. Annually he addresses thousands throughout the US and abroad on topics such as persevering leadership and community transformation.

Doug has received honorary and earned degrees from various colleges, including a PhD in Leadership and Human Development; a Doctorate of Humane Letters from Logos Graduate School; a Doctorate of Ministry from New Covenant International University, as well as a Pastoral Certificate in Practical Ministry from Regent University.

Somebody Cares has implemented several citywide strategies now multiplied in cities across the nation. Over the years, Somebody Cares has become a model for connecting needs with resources during natural calamities, including the Japan earthquake/tsunami, the Texas wildfires, the Haitian earthquake, the Indian Ocean tsunami, and

Hurricanes Katrina, Rita, and Ike. Through the expansion of the disaster preparedness and relief collaborations, the ministry has established the Global Compassion Response Network.

Doug has served on several disaster relief panels, including a forum hosted by the Heritage Foundation, based in Washington, DC. Doug served on the OneStar Foundation by appointment by the governor of Texas. He also serves on the international advisory board of the Geneva Institute for Leadership and Public Policy. He serves on various local, national, and international boards, including the Christian Men's Network and the Global Fatherhood Initiative. He serves as co-chair for the Billion Souls Initiative and for Mission America's Love2020 Initiative, as well as on the advisory boards of ministries such as Youth-Reach Houston, Coreluv for Orphans, Seniority Services, Inc., and others.

Doug served on the executive leadership committee of America for Jesus, a national prayer gathering held in Philadelphia. In August 2011, Doug served as national mobilization coordinator and Houston host for The Response, a national prayer gathering with approximately forty thousand people in attendance. He has also served as facilitator and moderator with Governor Bobby Jindal for The Response Louisiana; The Response South Carolina with Governor Nikki Haley; The Response North Carolina with Governor Pat McCrory; and The Response Florida with Governor Rick Scott.

Doug is the author of *It's Time to Cross the Jordan, The Fatherless Generation, Somebody Cares, Born to Die, Hope for the Fatherless Generation, Living Life Well,* and *In Search of a Father's Blessing.* His next book, *Leadership Awakening: Foundational Principles for Lasting Success,* will be released by Whitaker House in October 2016.

Doug, his wife, Lisa, and daughter, Ashley, reside in the greater Houston, Texas, area.